Fatally Flawed

The Sinful Reason Governments Fail

Martin R. Flowers

Contents

Introduction

We are a terminally ill nation. The symptoms of our collective illness are on display each day for the world to see. It is displayed through our actions towards others, violence, hatred, greed, jealousy, and lust. It is on display in our media, be it print, film, television or social. Our nation, for all of its superficial good, is at its core seeking to do harm. We are a terminally ill nation and the name of our affliction is sin.

That previous paragraph was one of the hardest I have ever written. I was raised in a family that is proud of our contributions to the United States of America. I was taught in school growing up that the United States of America is the best possible government people could have. But as the years have passed, I have come to the uncomfortable realization that something is very wrong with the nation I was raised to love. There is a deep disconnect between the spiritual teachings that formed the foundation of our nation and the actions our nation undertakes on a daily basis.

The goal of this book is to define the illness of sin that is plaguing the United States of America and how to cure it. While a lot of books on theology have taken different approaches to this topic, I want to tackle this topic from a different perspective. In the following pages we will look at what sin really is, why it matters in both a spiritual and physical sense, and why each of us should desire to address the sin in our lives. Finally, we will look at how sin impacts the government we have and how our perspective of sin creates many of the problems we are faced with in society today.

I will say up front that is will be a very different book from my previous offerings. In my two previous books I attempted to limit discussions of Christian theology in the body of the books and addressed those ideas in a post script. That will not be the case here as the reality of sin is completely tied to Christianity. No other religion on Earth has as its foundational premise that God took on the form of humans and give up that form to reconcile humanity to him on account of sin.

This book is intended to serve as a wake-up call of sorts to both believers and non-believers alike. While we can overcome sin by accepting

Christ, we will have a very difficult time living a victorious life as a follower of Christ if we are doing so in a childlike manner. It's far past time to grow up as believers and move beyond simple faith. This is not easy to do by any stretch of the imagination. Our society and cultures are such that anyone who professes Christ in this day and age is seen as mentally unstable and flawed. In this book I will go into detail about how this and other points of view adopted by our nation are the result of sin.

I want to be clear; this book is not about blaming anyone for sin. We have all sinned and we are all in need of repentance and salvation. The ability to seek repentance and find salvation is found solely in God's divine grace as demonstrated through Christ's sacrifice on the cross. Furthermore, being saved through the redemptive blood of Christ does not stop sin from occurring. My hope is that this book will help people to recognize the areas of their lives where sin manifests and how those sinful thoughts and behaviors interact and impact the government we desire. The government you want is the direct result of the sinful nature of your life. The person who is actively embracing sin will want a government that seeks to care for them so they are never responsible for themselves. The person who has accepted

Christ will seek after a government of limited ability, realizing that God is the ultimate governing authority and that any attempt humans make at government will result in sinful defeat. The reason believers seek after limited government is that the Holy Spirit has impressed upon every believer, whether they realize it or not, that all governments are sinful. The act of creating a government is always a sinful response to the sinful acts of sinful people.

In part one of this book we will explore what the sin nature is as a foundation for the rest of our discussion. We will look at what sin is and why sin is bad. Let's face it, there are a lot of people in the world today who live happy lives while in sin. It's becoming more and more common for our society to openly accept sin. Truth be told, many of the people our society lifts up on a pedestal are openly embracing sinful lifestyles. We will look at how sin is impacting our individual relationship with God and how God views our humanity and our sin nature. We'll finish by looking at why God sent his son, Jesus Christ, to die for our sins. The fact is, that we as a species must hold a lot of importance to God for him to make such a tremendous sacrifice.

In part two of this book we will look at the nature of our government and how it is impacted by the sinful behavior of citizens. In my first book *Null and Void* I demonstrated the failure of the United States government to fulfil the obligations laid out in the preamble to the U.S. Constitution. For those of you who read *Null and Void* some of this material will seem, as we will go back and reexamine the concepts found in the preamble of the United States Constitution. This part of the book will be examining the sinful underpinnings that have resulted in those failures, and why our government will never be successful in accomplishing those goals. We will also explore the realization that just because you have a government made up of "good people who have been saved" does not mean that it will be a good government. We will examine the concept of self-government and whether a "…government of the people, by the people, and for the people…" is realistic given the sinful nature of humanity and ask the question: is the concept of government sinful? When we as humans seek to institute our own forms of government, are we in essence telling God that we can do it better than He can?

In part three we will reexamine my writings in *Governance by Addiction*, the nature of partisan politics and how sin impacts the political beliefs of non-believers. We will look at how the addict thought process that I detailed as driving the political left is influenced by the sin nature. We will explore why people struggling with sin often find themselves drawn towards liberal ideologies. Is there some innate aspect of modern liberalism that makes it more easily swayed by the effects of sin? What is it about the liberal ideology that draws people in and how does sin play a role? We will also take a hard look at the main reason liberalism is diametrically opposed to Christianity and why liberals are determined to force Christians from the public sphere.

Finally, we'll finish with a discussion of some good news. I once heard a co-worker refer to me as "the most chill person I've ever met". I have worked at a number of jobs over the years where my life was in danger daily. I have lost count of how many times I have had someone threaten to kill me. Despite all of the chaos, violence and sin that has surrounded me every day, I have lived without anxiety, fear or concerns. I often hear liberals talk of wanting to create a "safe space", so in the conclusion to this book I will invite you into my safe space. As humans we are not forced to live in fear, we make the choice to live there.

As with any book discussing politics and social issues, there are going to be some difficult subjects discussed. As a nation we have faced difficult times, and continue to unfortunately struggle with the results of some past mistakes. My sincere hope is that as we journey through the following chapters were can begin to see a path forward to correcting past mistakes and creating a better future for our nation.

Chapter 1: What is Sin?

Before we can begin discussing the solution to the disease our nation is facing, we must first begin by looking into the disease process itself. As a society we tend to have a very twisted view of sin. Part of this is the result of the Ten Commandments, part of this is the result of sin itself. We are typically taught that sin is a specific act. The Old Testament version of sin was murder, adultery, stealing, lying, etc. In reality the world itself is sin and all of those acts we identify as "sin" are just the manifestation of the sinful world we have created. The world that God created was perfect, but when we as humans turned away from the will of God and towards our own selfish desires, we created the sin that tainted God's creation and remade God's perfect creation into the world we have today.

As humans we also have a tendency to make sin personal. We hold onto sins that we commit and we hold grudges about sins committed against us. I've seen people hold onto sins for decades and watched as it slowly eroded away

their life as they continued to dwell on a previous wrong. We see this in politics, where a politician will engage in some ill-conceived behavior and it continues to be brought up time and again. Worst yet is when we refuse to accept that we have sinned and continue to act as if it never happened. In the most extreme cases we like to point out other
people's sins, because it draws attention away from our own. In many of these cases we are simply projecting our own sinful nature onto others.

   Imagine sin as the water in an ocean we're all floating in but we're forbidden from ingesting any of the water. Sin is exactly the same way; we are surrounded by sin and in some cases, we have no choice but to commit sinful acts as a result. This is the irony of the question "why does God allow bad things to happen to good people?" I've yet to meet one of these mythical good people. None of us are perfect and none of us are without sin. Every person who has reached adulthood has sinned at some point in their life. Anything that serves no other purpose but to separate us from God is a sin. The goal of life is to become closer to God and to help others achieve the same. When we follow after worldly ideals and beliefs, we work to build a wall between ourselves and God.

In the simplest of terms, sin is at the very core of our earthly existence. To break free from the enslavement of sin we must learn to break free from our world of sin. Left to our own devices we will inevitably seek what is sinful over what is spiritual. The sinful elements of the world are those that feed our own selfish desires. We cannot of our own free will break free from those selfish desires, no matter how hard we try. Sin is like the worst form of quicksand a person can get stuck in. The further the individual goes into sin, the harder it becomes to pull yourself out of it. To make matters worse, society is made up of sinful people so inevitably society will descend into the same sinful problems. Of all societies where this will happen, a democracy is the worst.

While growing up we are told that a democracy is the best possible government we can have. We look around and we see all the choices that we have and pride ourselves on what we have the freedom to do. However, there is a very ugly side to democracy. The same freedom of choice that drives millions of people to choose to give money to help victims of a natural disaster also drives an individual to carry out a mass shooting. The sad truth is that all the sins of the world are not only manifested, but magnified, in a democracy. Choice is not a good thing when you live in a world full of sin and you have a natural tendency to make bad choices.

So why does sin have so much power over us? Because we let it! The nature of sin is that it has an addictive quality. But it's different from the addiction to drugs or alcohol. Sin's addiction is not based on chemical dependency but on a desire to avoid the feelings sin generates. Sin creates this twisted circle where we commit sins to avoid the sins we've already committed. To make it worse, since we live in a sinful world, we have no choice but to sin at times. Since the dawn of humanity people have sought different ways to deal with sin and its effect on us individually and as a society. There are a number of popular ways of escaping from sin. Some people throw themselves into work or relationships. Some people turn to drugs and alcohol. Some people use hobbies to distract themselves from sin. This is not to say that having hobbies, being in a relationship or working is bad. However, when these are used as an addictive means of avoiding the sinful nature of life these tend to cause problems. Given enough time, all sin will result in some form of addiction. We naturally want to run away from our sinful behaviors and when we find a means of accomplishing this, we develop a pattern of behaviors that allow us to continue that activity, no matter how destructive it might be. This is the essence of addiction.

In societal terms we try to deal with sin by creating government and laws. We hope in vain that by creating laws we can legislate sin out of existence. We hope that by making murder illegal that it will make the sinful act of murder go away, but it doesn't. In some cases, we get so desperate that we try to restrict the ability of sin to function in our world. Laws regarding drugs and alcohol, gun control, sex and many others are the result of foolish attempts to control sin. These attempts never work, but in our sinful state we convince ourselves otherwise and continue to try regardless.

It's also sin that drives us away from God and the only means we have to cure ourselves of the disease. This is where sin does its best work. Despite what we are led to believe, sin is not the creation of Satan, and it's certainly not the creation of God. Sin is of our own creation. What I mean by this is that each person creates the sin they are dealing with in some way, shape or form. In many ways Mary Shelley was trying to convey this idea in her classic novel *Frankenstein*. Dr. Frankenstein's monster was of his own creation, but once it was created, he found himself powerless to stop it. To that end,

Dr. Frankenstein dies in a distant, cold place having chased his own sin there. How many of us have followed after Victor Frankenstein without realizing it? To make matters worse we follow one sinful act with another, and another and another, until we reach a point where sin is so compounded that we feel we will never be able to recover.

This leads to the inevitable questions: is all sin the same? Yes, all sin is the same. For all the horrible things that happen in the world, it's hard to believe this, but all sins are the same. No sin is worse than any other. The genesis of all sin is the same selfish beliefs. The murderer is no worse in reality than the husband cheating on his wife. We might see the murderer as worse, but it's actually our sin nature that acts as the driving force behind that belief. While we create our own sin, it is God who gets to define what sin is. From God's view
point, a sin is anything that draws you away from His glory and blessings. That is a very broad view of sin I'll grant you, but it's true. Almost all that we do in life is seen as sinful and at times that can seem depressing, as though we can't escape the impact of sin on our lives. This is part of the power sin has over our lives, to cause us to do what we otherwise would not do. In desperation to escape our sinful decisions we

will inevitably make other sinful decisions and continue to do so until we are forced to come to terms with the original sinful decision we made. And all of those sinful decisions are focused on preventing us from inevitably being forced to deal with the consequences of our sins.

All sin has to be the same because more than just God's defining of sin, we have the way it impacts our lives. All sin leads to the same destructive path. All sin results in consequences that we wish to avoid. Part of the problem humanity has in terms of dealing with sin is seeing sin as existing on a scale. This view of sin is based on the impact the sin has on others and not on the person who commits the sin in the first place. The true damage caused by sin is not on the person who the sin is committed against as it is the damage to the person who commits the sin. This view of sin is not however consistent with what the Bible teaches about sin. This view is consistent with how we see crimes, that murder is worse than robbery. However, when we look at the Ten Commandments, we see that God placed murder much further down the list then our society does. As humans we have a natural desire, fueled by sin, to rationalize and categorize the world around us. As a result, we seek to rationalize sin as opposed to accepting our own involvement with the existence of sin.

One of the reasons we rationalize sin is because our sins are always the result of our own decisions. The problem is that we are often times making decisions based on our own sinful desires over what is actually best for us and the people around us. Over the last few years, we've heard of an increasing number of pastors of major churches across the United States who have been forced to step away from their duties due to sinful practices. I doubt that any of those individuals went into the ministry thinking that they were going to succumb to the temptations of sin. I have every confidence that they came out of school with the best of intentions to spread the good news of Christ and help their fellow humans come to know God more deeply. However, somewhere along the way things went wrong. I think people who work in ministry have a heavy burden in that they are faced with the nature of sin every day. They see people who are living a life embracing sin and being successful. It is only natural that some of them slip and go down the wrong path.

The problem becomes compounded when they begin to rationalize their actions. We don't rationalize good decisions, because there is no need to. That is a concept I always use when

I'm getting ready to make a decision, I ask myself: how would I explain this decision to someone else? When you start looking at how you would explain a decision to someone else, you come to realize if you are rationalizing a bad decision. Particularly if you use phrases like "it was the right thing to do because…", "it was for the best…" or "I had no other choice than to…". These are the kind of qualifying statements we use to make the decision sound better, but really those types of phrases show that we're not comfortable with the decision we made. The problem is made even worse because the rationalization marginalizes those we love and care for. The pastor who has an affair is not only hurting himself, but is also hurting his wife, children, friends, church and the body of Christ in general.

Sin has more ability to destroy human life than any disease known to humanity. You can find the most virulent virus in the world today, and it lacks the ability to cause a fraction of the damage sin can cause in a single moment in time. Sins ability to radiate into other parts of our lives and the lives of those around us is unparalleled. For this reason, it is incredibly important that we understand what sin is and how to successfully confront it.

Chapter 2: Why is Sin Important?

When I was a student in college, I decided to take a course in human evolution just to see what all the controversy was about. While taking the class I began to contemplate the way God created humans. I began to ask God for clarity about how creation happened. I realized early on in the course that much of the evidence I was being shown was open to interpretation and that the view many scientists were adopting had more to do with their own sense of bounded rationality than with any actual scientific fact.

As I considered the subject matter, I began to read the creation narrative from Genesis again. Genesis 1:26 states "And God said, Let us make man in our image, after our likeness…". This line struck me as odd, what did God mean by the words "image" and "likeness"? The more I prayed on the issue the answer came to me, we are created in God's likeness. Clearly God did not mean in His physical image, as there would be no need for God to say this since no human would know the physical appearance of God until Christ was born. However, we are created in God's likeness, which means we are three separate parts in one being just as God is three separate parts in one being. Now I want to be very careful here in explaining this. By no means am I implying that humans are in any way divine. Humans are not "little gods" like Word of Faith doctrine teaches. Humans are not gods destined to rule over a planet for eternity as the LDS church teaches. Humans are created in God's perfect image. That image includes an eternal soul, a flesh and blood body and a Holy Spirit. While not an exact reflection of the Trinity, God clearly was drawing on His own perfect likeness when He created humans.

So, what does being created in the likeness of God mean for us? The way God created humans tells us some important truths about how we came to be where we are today. It matters because the composition of each person is what determines the extent of their life. For someone to live they must possess two of those three elements. You can continue to live as long as you have some combination of soul, body and spirit. In the beginning God created Adam and Eve in this likeness, a perfect representation of Himself. However, once sin entered into the equation there was a change.

The Holy Spirit is incapable of existing within the sin nature. The Holy Spirit is the extension of God's truth, and it cannot exist in the presence of lies. It's like oil and water, there is a natural separation between these two aspects of our being. As stated earlier, you must have a minimum of two of the three elements to live. The soul is eternal, so you cannot lose that. However, you can lose the Holy Spirit as a result of sin and you can lose the physical body as a result of natural processes, injury or disease. For a person who is bound in slavery to their sin nature, they are existing as only the soul and the body. Once their body fails, they will die. However, for the person who is in Christ, they have been freed from their sin state and have the Holy Spirit residing in them. Thus, when their body fails, they are left with the soul and the spirit and continue to live.

This might seem like a foreign idea to many, including Christians because it's not taught in churches. However, when we look to the scriptures, we find clear evidence for this. In John 19:30 Christ's death on the Cross is described as follows "When Jesus had received the sour wine, he said, "It is finished," and he bowed his head and gave up his spirit." There are two parts clearly described in His death on the Cross. First, He "bowed his head" indicating the death of the physical body. Second, he "gave up his spirit" indicating that the Holy Spirit was separated from his body. Thus, left with only His eternal being, Christ was truly dead.

This view of Christ's death on the Cross provides further evidence for the "Harrowing of Hell" as described in 1 Peter. If the Holy Spirit cannot exist in the presence of sin, then it only makes sense that the eternal being of the Godhead would need to be separated from the Holy Spirit before Christ could enter into hell. We see this further illustrated in John 7:37 "But this spake he of the Spirit, which they that believe on him should receive: for the Holy Ghost was not yet given; because that Jesus was not yet glorified." Christ's glorification appears to have occurred only after the descent into Hell and His resurrection on the third day. The fact that Christ said "It is finished" on the Cross not only indicates that the sin debt has been "paid in full" but also serves to denote that there was nothing Satan could do at that juncture to prevent Christ's inevitable victory over sin and death.

This point is further illustrated in John 20:21-23 where we have an important exchange that occurs:

> Then said Jesus to them again, Peace be
> unto you: as my Father hath sent me,
> even so send I you. And when he had
> said this, he breathed on them, and saith
> unto them, receive ye the Holy
> Ghost: Whose so ever sins ye remit, they
> are remitted unto them; and whose so
> ever sins ye retain, they are retained.

This passage is highly important because it parallels Genesis 2:7:

> And the Lord God formed man of the dust
> of the ground, and breathed into his
> nostrils the breath of life; and man
> became a living soul.

This passage in Genesis 2:7 is indicative of two key ideas. First, that the Holy Spirit is included in the breath of life. Prior to God breathing into Adam, his body was not alive. Once God breathed into him, Adam became a "living soul". This again confirms that we need two of the three elements, Soul, Body and Spirit, to be alive. Secondly, it shows the need to be "born again" as Christ described in John 3. Christ, being God incarnate, breathed life anew into His followers.

We also must remember that Christ was not concerned with saving the body. Christ even states as much in Matthew 10:28 "And fear not them which kill the body, but are not able to kill the soul: but rather fear him which is able to destroy both soul and body in hell." Later in Matthew 16:26 when Christ said "For what is a man profited, if he shall gain the whole world, and lose his own soul? Or what shall a man give in exchange for his soul?" Our earthly bodies are corrupted by sin, and while salvation in the form of accepting Christ allows us to be rejoined with the Holy Spirit, it is not a substitute for the replacement of God's perfect creation. Once in God's heavenly kingdom we will receive new, incorruptible bodies. This concept is made clear by Paul in 1 Corinthians 15:51-53:

> Behold, I shew you a mystery; We shall not all sleep, but we shall all be changed, In a moment, in the twinkling of an eye, at the last trump: for the trumpet shall sound, and the dead shall be raised incorruptible, and we shall be changed. For this corruptible must put on incorruption, and this mortal must put on immortality.

Clearly, God intends for us to take on new bodies, so why be concerned with the corrupted body we currently have?

Some people are going to argue at this point that none of this can be true because Christ retook His body after his resurrection. However, Christ's body was not corrupted. Going back to

Genesis 6 we see a very important task that God undertook that many believers miss. Genesis 6:8-9 reads:

> But Noah found grace in the eyes of the Lord. These are the generations of Noah: Noah was a just man and perfect in his generations, and Noah walked with God.

The words "perfect in his generations" is very important when we see that Noah is listed in the genealogy of Christ found in Luke 3:36. Since the Garden of Eden, Satan has sought to prove humans as being an inferior creation. Part of Satan's plan to accomplish this was to corrupt the genetic material along the line that would lead to Christ[1]. To this end Satan sent his fellow fallen angels to corrupt the genetic material and prevent Christ from being the perfect sacrifice for our sins as described in both Leviticus and Numbers as being "without blemish". By destroying all human life except for Noah and his family, God was able to abolish the genetic damage that Satan had done and ensure the line that Christ was descending from was "without blemish".

---

[1] I'll admit that I'm not sure why this was important as Christ was born of a virgin and the genetic line discussed here is being traced through Joseph who was not Jesus' biological father. I suspect it has something to do with Mosaic laws and customs and Christ being descended from the House of David.

This is what drives us to "fix" sin, because we know on some level that we must repair our relationship with God to stay alive. The human body as God created it is marvelous. For example, when injured the body will begin to undertake certain processes to maintain life. In cases of people with hypothermia we see the body shifting warmth to the core of the body at the detriment of the extremities to preserve life. When people are placed in a situation that is dangerous it triggers the "fight or flight" response. Our body also drives us to do something similar in response to our sin nature. The problem is that those natural defenses are corrupted by sin in the absence of the Holy Spirit. Let's face it, it is much easier to accept sin or rationalize sinful behavior than to accept responsibility for our actions and deal with the consequences. If you get a speeding ticket as a teenager you would much rather your parent not find out about it because you know there will be consequences when they do. But eventually they will find out, because you're probably going to need money to pay the fine and your car insurance is going to go up. When your parents do find out the punishment will be a lot worse because not only were you speeding, but you failed to come clean about it.

This example shows how our desire to rationalize and justify our sinful actions and beliefs leads us further into sin. We do this because we know on some level that left uncorrected that same sin will prevent us from living eternally. This is where many of our emotions come from. Our emotions are often the result of the anxiety we feel when faced with the eternal consequences of our sins. We then allow our emotions to convince ourselves that the best thing to do is to just get away from the problem. Instead of dealing with the sinful nature of who we are, we seek to run away from dealing with the issue. Inevitably in running away from sin we end up creating more sin in our lives and we run away from that also. Some people run their entire lives and never deal with their sin nature. Some people run until their sin nature catches up with them. And some people end up being destroyed by their sins because they refuse to face them. In chapter one I mentioned Mary Shelley's character Dr. Frankenstein, and this is exactly what he did. Dr. Frankenstein chased his sinful monster until he ultimately destroyed himself. Left unresolved, sin will always result in spiritual self-destruction. This shouldn't surprise us; this is what sin does. Expecting sin to not destroy you is like expecting a lion not to eat a gazelle. The goal is to limit the destructive capability sin has in our lives.

Chapter 3: Staging the Disease

There are many people who have read the two previous chapters and said "okay, we might have a problem with sin, but is it really that bad?" The answer is an emphatic yes. Everywhere we turn in modern society we see the evidence of the state of moral decay created by our own sinful nature on display. To make matters worse we have taken to accepting much of this as a norm as a result of cognitive dissidence. The problem has gotten so bad that our society openly attacks anyone for pointing out the moral short comings of society. While there are any number of examples that show how far we have drifted as a society from God's ideal, there are a few that highlight the problem better than others.

The amount of bullying that takes place in our society is getting much worse. Bullying has always been a problem associated with sin for a number of different reasons. One person will always seek to impose their will on another person. However, the ability for people to carry out these types of attacks in anonymity is new to our modern society. This is very emblematic of sin, because it allows for the sin not just to linger in the person who is committing it but to be spread to others. Sin thrives on the ability to infect others because it makes sin seem more acceptable the more people are infected. This is a reason sin is driven by anonymity, because sin acts like a virus that can spread when people are asymptomatic. The anonymity of the internet allows people to engage in all kind of sinful behavior without the fear of being caught. We see this nowhere more clearly than on the "dark web" where people are allowed to engage in all kinds of sinful and illegal activity in anonymity. The more anonymity a person has the more likely they are to do things they don't want others to know about.

What makes this new era of bullying more sinful is that it's often used to attack what is true. The bullies have taken to attacking others in the name of "social justice" in the hope that no one will realize that they are bullies. Now anyone who disagrees with the sinful acts that society is openly endorsing is referred to as a racist, bigot, misogynist, or any other of a number of different hateful stereotypes which aren't necessarily true. While there are actual acts of racism, bigotry and other types of hate in the world, there are cases where those terms are used by bullies to silence freedom of speech and expression. There are a lot of people in the world who I don't agree with their opinions and beliefs, but I still respect their right to have those opinions and beliefs. In essence the bullies are now trying to bully people into believing that other people are bullies…and a whole lot of people are falling for it.

This is how sin behaves as an addiction. Sin seeks to lay the blame for all the wrongs a person has engaged in on someone else. Anyone who has read my previous books will recognize this as one of the last stages of liberalism as described in *Governance by Addiction*. When forced to face the consequences of their addiction the addict will seek to blame others for the problem and sin is no different. How many times have we heard a husband or wife who cheated on their spouse make excuses for why they cheated? The goal is to make the infidelity seem okay since it was justified by some action the spouse took. In reality, this poor attempt at blaming others is simple a person's desire to avoid the full consequences of their own sinful behavior. We see this in some cases of police brutality. While there can be little doubt that police officers do at times step over the line on occasion, there are also cases where criminals claim police brutality as a means of covering for their own criminal actions. If someone commits a crime and resists arrest, then they should expect that officers will need to get more physical in their response.

Another area where we see sin controlling our society is in our forms of entertainment. As our society edges closer to the sinful abyss, we see our entertainment becoming more sexual and violent. Our nation's most popular television shows feature violence at an alarming rate. If federal agents killed as many people in real life as they do on television there would be congressional investigations. Despite this many of our elected officials are more worried about lining their campaign coffers with donations from the entertainment industry instead of safeguarding the morality of our nation. This has resulted in an entire generation of people who have been raised to believe that the solution to life's problems can be found in the barrel of a gun. Thus, when things start to go wrong, they reach for a gun. To make matters worse society acts surprised when violence and mass shootings happen. The inevitable reaction that follows is to blame the shooter, or a firearms manufacturer for the events. No one ever bothers to ask what went wrong in the shooters life to create the conditions that resulted to those tragic events. The media loves to demonize the gunman in those kinds of incidents because it's easy to do. The reality is that the gunman is just carrying out the execution sentence the jury has handed down and if you want to face the jury look in the mirror. While it does not in any way excuse the actions of the shooter, it is imperative that we understand that the collective sinful actions of society that drove someone to that point.

By creating this notion that violence is the solution to life's problems it also ingrains in people the idea that those problems are someone else's and not their own. The more the entertainment industry reinforces the idea that violence, and particularly violence aimed at an external source of aggravation, is the answer to the problem, sin will continue to reign in people's lives. Instead of addressing the problem of violence being caused by sin and the entertainment industry fueling our sin nature, politicians look to band firearms. This is simply one more way that sin twists our mentality and perspective.

One very popular means of society accepting sin is seen in the LGBTQ movement. I know this is a very unpopular topic, but I simply cannot ignore it. The entire LGBTQ movement is founded on a series of made up words designed to falsely convey a sense of legitimacy to an argument that lacks any logical defense. There are no "homosexuals". The word "homosexual" means a person who is capable of reproducing through sexual relations with a member of the same sex. Science has told us that this is not possible within the human race. And by that same logic there are no "bisexuals". A person's sex, the biological means by which they reproduce, is not determined by a doctor or society; it's determined by the composition of the person's 46th chromosome. This also means that there is no way to do a "sex change surgery". Such a medical procedure would require the transmogrification of the 46th chromosome from XX to XY or vise-versa. If the medical community ever discovers a way to change DNA, I would hope it would be used to cure cancer and not to change a person's sex.

The term "transgender" has nothing to do with sexuality. Gender is the roles that society places on people and are passed down to each successive generation through enculturation. Gender roles tend to be fluid, and change with the needs of a society. For example, during World War Two when many men in the U.S. were engaged in fighting, women were required to take on many gender roles that were traditionally assigned to men. Furthermore, people cannot have "gender reassignment surgery" as it's an oxymoronic statement. Since gender has no basis in biology, there is no way the medical community can perform "surgery" to change what a person's gender is. If a person feels like they are a woman trapped inside of a man's body, then they have a body image disorder and the answer is psychological counseling and not body modification surgery. If a person with anorexia claimed that they were a fat person trapped inside of a skinny person's body would we approve of them having gastric bypass surgery? Absolutely not, so why is it different for issues of sexuality and gender?

Now I want to be clear, there are actual medical conditions people can be born with that create uncertainty about sexuality, but these conditions are rare. The LBGTQ community and their supporters are insulting people who actually have these conditions. People who have legitimate medical conditions that result in unclear sexuality are being marginalized by a group of people who are seeking to either run from their sins or actively live in sin.

Finally, I want to discuss one of the areas in our society where sin lives without fear: churches. I know that last sentence came as a surprise to many readers but it's true. There was a time in our nation where churches were the cornerstones of our communities. However, as our nation has grown our churches have taken a backseat in many communities and when people do attend it's more out of a sense of societal obligation thane because they love God. For many people church attendance is just part of their social calendar, no different than attending the high school football game on Friday night or the country club for a round of golf on Saturday afternoon. The late Rev. Billy Graham once said many professing Christian spend their week "sowing wild oats and then show up in church on Sunday morning praying for a crop failure", and he's right.

The fact that we have taken to treating church as a social club over a place to worship God is further compounding the problem. This notion of a church being a place for social gatherings has created a growing number of issues. First, it has given rise to the "mega church" culture, where people can go to church while remaining anonymous. Remember back in chapter 2 when I mentioned that sin loves anonymity? Well, sin loves anonymity in no place more than in the church. God never intended for the church to exist in anonymity. During his ministry Jesus was very aware of this and required people to make a very public confession of faith in Him.

The anonymity found in the mega churches gives cover for a lot of sinful behavior. In a mega church people can cheat on their spouse or develop problems with drugs and alcohol and it quite possibly goes unnoticed. If these same things occurred in a small community church the pastor and church elders would be stepping in to say something. When allowed to continue uncheck sin will infect the entire church. Paul warned of this in 1st Corinthians 15:33 "Be not deceived: evil communications corrupt good manners."

   The second issue we see occurring in churches is what I call "Buffet Line Christianity". This is where the church cherry picks what parts of the Christian faith they want to talk about. These churches want to talk a lot about ideas such as grace, forgiveness, salvation and blessings. But they avoid the concepts of judgment, sin and damnation like they were the plague. This type of faith provides openings for sin to weaken and eventually destroy your faith. Faith is an all or nothing proposition. When we pick what we're going to believe it ceases to be faith and becomes a matter of personal philosophy. This is because when we pick to only believe certain elements of a belief, then we have the option of choosing to believe only the ideas that we can prove, or the beliefs that we like. Then suddenly adultery is no longer a sin, and drug use is okay. Before long we end up with pastors preaching that Christ's death wasn't real and that we don't really need salvation. Those clearly are not ideas consistent with Christian beliefs. We cannot allow sin to dictate our faith, we must allow God to dictate our faith through the indwelling of the Holy Spirit.

The third problem is churches "Prostituting the Bride of Christ". This is where churches are willing to look the other way to add money to their bank account. A perfect example of this is marriage. While it has become common for marriage to occur between any two people that the courts deem fit, the truth of the matter is far different. If we look to the book of Genesis to when God created marriage, we see that this was done before sin entered into the world. The truth is that only two persons free from the slavery of sin can be married in the eyes of God. No matter what the courts, be those legal or of public opinion, may say on the matter, God is the ultimate arbitrator of His divine creation and since God created marriage, it is God's decision what constitutes marriage. Now if a couple wishes to get "married" in a secular sense, that's fine, but go to a park, a courthouse, or other public venue, not a Christian church. Simply stated, my faith in Christ and his finished work at the Cross does not exist so that someone else can accomplish their fairy tale wedding. If that kind of activity were undertaken towards any other segment of our society it would be labeled as "cultural misappropriation" and lambasted by social justice warriors on social media. However, since a sizable segment of our society has determined that mistreating Christians is okay, no one says anything.

Despite this realization, we see churches willing to rent out the building, and in some cases even pastors willing to officiate, for weddings of couples who intend to continue in sin. Is it not enough that our faith in Christ is under constant attack in the secular world? Do we really need to provide them a pulpit within our houses of worship to further attack our faith? Our fight as a church against sin in this world is tough to begin with, and would be impossible if not for Christ's sacrifice at the Cross. It feels like we are handing victories to sin in these battles and the reason is that churches are focusing on secular instead of spiritual goals. And while it might be easy to say that this is just a few isolated incidents, the more those incidents occur the more of a habit we form as a church, and before long it becomes the norm. Sin wants nothing more than for the default setting for every human to be following after sin.

Chapter 4: The Truth Shall Set You Free

Having come to the realization that our own sins are the source of our problems; we need to discuss the answer: Jesus Christ. There are people out there who will make every attempt to disprove this book based simply on this chapter, because they insist there are multiple ways to eternal life. Simply put, they are wrong. The only means of curing the disease of sin is found in Christ's completed work at the cross. It is the result of his completed work at the Cross that allows us to remove the harmful effects of sin on our lives and restore the Holy Spirit in our lives. Without the Holy Spirit being restored in a person's live, nothing else matters. In John 14 Christ said "I am the Way, the Truth and the Life, and no one shall enter the House of my Father except by Me…". This line of scripture is a favorite at funerals, but few Christians take the time to think on its true meaning. All three parts of the statement are self-evident. Christ is the way to salvation, Christ is the means of eternal life, and as "the word made flesh" Christ was the embodiment of truth.

We need to remove the influence of sin within a person's life because it impacts their concept of truth. Before sending Christ to be crucified, Pontus Pilate famously asked Christ "What is truth?" In order for truth to exist there must be an all-powerful being that is capable of seeing everything that has ever happened, everything that is currently happening and everything that ever will happen. We call this omnipotent, omniscient and omnipresent being God. From this realization we learn that truth is the view of the eternal universe from the perspective of God. However, our sin nature prevents us from understanding that God is the source of all truth, and as a result drives us to follow after false "truths" that will lead you further into sin.

Without an understanding that God is the source of all truth you slip into a form of spiritual schizophrenia where your perceptions of truth become twisted by a form of relativism defined by you and not truth. This occurs because as humans we live in a condition known as bounded rationality, where it is impossible for us to know the truth about every situation we encounter. Where we see this most powerfully is with racism. In racism we see people who form their own "truths" based on events relative to their own life and not God. As a result, the racist person will begin to create "truths" in order to rationalize their flawed beliefs. The same is true of people who want to claim everyone who stands in opposition to their beliefs is a racist. This is the root cause of the identity politics that are paralyzing our nation.

Our own sinful behavior causes us to create our own "truths" as opposed to accepting the truth of God. The result of creating our own "truths" only makes the sin worse. It becomes this downward spiral where the sin results in more sin. Ultimately the only thing a person has left in their life is the sin they have created and the reality of the world around them seems like fiction. This idea should sound familiar; in the media we call it "fake news". The news media has taken to reporting the truth they have created as opposed to what is really happening in the world.

The realization that God is the source of all truth is critical to everything that follows. Having established that God is truth, we can be assured that God cannot lie. For the truth to be a lie would create a paradox that would unravel all of reality. If there is no truth then everything would potentially be a lie rendering it impossible to distinguish reality from fantasy. Imagine what the world would be like if everyone lived in their own fantasy world with different rules. The rule of law would cease to exist and society would crumble.

This also provides us with proof that the God's word is inerrant. I want to make a very distinct point here regarding the Bible as being the inerrant word of God. The word of God as dictated to the original writers of the Bible was inerrant. However, since the original text was written there have been hundreds of translations, most of which are different. Just because someone claims a particular book is The Bible, does not make it the true word of God. The truth is there are translations of the Bible in the world that encourage adultery, killing children and all kinds of other vices. There is nothing to say what does or does not constitute the Bible. While various churches have developed particular biblical canon over the years, not even these completely agree. The Bible for the Roman Catholic Church and the Bible for a Southern Baptist Church might look the same but contain some very different ideas. This is the ultimate example of never judging a book by its cover. Just because a book has the title Holy Bible on the cover does not mean it is the word of God.

So where does this leave the human race? It leaves us with a very uncomfortable realization, that our sin nature prevents us from knowing the truth that is found in God. This is uncomfortable because our soul wants to be closer to God, but the sinful world we live in wants to drive us further away from God. Sometimes the truth is scary, and accepting the truth requires us to comfort uncomfortable feelings. This truth reveals one of the most uncomfortable feelings you will ever experience, and that is the feeling of losing control. As humans we have to come to terms with the realization that we are not in control of the world around us, and that God ultimately is. Furthermore, as much as humanity might try, we can never know the truth as long as we are separated from God. In order to restore our relationship with God we must atone for our sin nature and reestablish the link with God that is formed through the Holy Spirit. Once we are free from the slavery of sin and death, we can know the truth. God wants us to know the truth, that is why he sent Christ to die for our sins.

Earlier I mentioned the idea of sin being a massive ocean we are all floating in and the Cross serving as the lifesaver God has thrown to us. What makes grabbing that lifesaver difficult is that the water is cold and impairs our thinking. Sin clouds our judgment and causes us to do things we know we shouldn't do and it causes us to not do things we know we should do. Then to make matters worse, sin will make us believe that we don't need redemption and that we should go on living in sin regardless of what we know to be true. This is how sin goes about creating "truth" from lies. The false truth that is created by our sin nature will drive us to engage in behavior that causes us to commit more sins and serves to drive us further from God.

Sin wears us down overtime. As sin works to wear you down, you develop a form of cognitive dissidence, where your sin state becomes the new norm. Sin will also drive you to turn away from people who are not as sinful, because being around them becomes "uncomfortable". In some really extreme cases the person will develop a false rationalization for pushing people away where their soul wants the opposite. Sinfulness will always push a person towards sin and the souls will push a person towards righteousness. In this way the body and the soul act as positive and negative charges, except instead of drawing the opposite to them, they draw the same charge and repel the opposite. Sin will even drive people to rationalize not accepting Christ because of all the pain it will leave them feeling. Accepting Christ is not easy by any means. Christ himself warned us to "count the cost". Christ went even further to provide us with the Parable of the Sower to demonstrate this truth. Each of the growing conditions that Christ described can be found in the life of believers. We've all seen or heard of believers who based on outward appearances had a very strong relationship with Christ. However, once a major tragedy befell them, their faith crumbed. In these cases, we see individuals who desire the social appearance and self-gratification that came with being seen as a successful part of a church community, but they were unwilling to put in the hard work of developing a deep and lasting relationship with Christ.

Let's look back at the earlier analogy of sin being like an ocean. Just like in life, it's easy to avoid ingesting any of the water when the water is calm and there are no waves. However, the time is going to come when a storm will be on the horizon and the wind will blow and the waves will build. In that moment is will be virtually impossible to not ingest some of the water. Not everyone's storm will look the same. Some people will be brought down by sins associated with a minor squall and some of us will be laid low be a thunderous hurricane. We will all face the temptations of sin, Christ even admitted as much in Matthew 18:7 when he said "Woe unto the world because of offences! for it must needs be that offences come…".

Since the world is awash in sin, how can we overcome it? We overcome the world by removing ourselves from the influences of the world. This does not mean that we remove ourselves from the world, for even Christ himself prayed that the Father would protect us in the world but not remove us from it. If we were to remove ourselves from the world, then our light would not shine to lead others to salvation through Christ. However, this does mean that we cannot live in this world as if it is our eternal home. The desire for worldly possessions and worldly power will drive a person to stray further away from faith in God and closer to the sinful nature of the world.

Does this mean that we must live in isolation from the world around us? Absolutely not! Living in the spirit means being mindful of the reality of the sinful world around us but realizing that the sinful world we are in is only temporary and that the gift of salvation is forever. Part of what makes sin bad is that sin diverts or shortens our journey to know Christ. In other words, sin occurs when you take your eyes off the eternal prize! Adultery, sex outside of marriage and aberrant sexual relations are sinful because it places emphasis on lust over the will of God. Murder, be it criminal or state sanctioned, is a sin because it cuts short the ability of someone to come to know Christ and to do God's work. Greed is a sin because it places the emphasis on our own personal goals over the goals of God. All sin comes down to a very simple decision that we all make at some point in our lives: are we going to be selfless or selfish?

Selfishness is what drives virtually all of the sin in our world. On some level every action that is inherently sinful is also selfish. To make matters worse, the selfish person will never want to fully accept God's gift of salvation offered through His Son because of their own pride, yet another sin. In Matthew 12 Christ told that the only unforgivable sin is blasphemy of the Holy Spirit. The reason for this sin being unforgivable is rooted in the nature of sin itself. God will freely forgive any sin, and sent His Son to die for all sins. However, the person who blasphemies the Holy Spirit is so selfish that they will never ask for forgiveness for the sin they are committing.

Sin originates with people wanting to live in the world and follow after other sins. Where selfishness is the true root of all evil, it's the sinful world that provides the fuel that drives selfishness to exist. I'm reminded of the words of Christ in Matthew 16:24-26:
Then said Jesus unto his disciples, If

any man will come after me, let him deny himself, and take up his cross, and follow me. For whosoever will save his life shall lose it: and whosoever will lose his life for my sake shall find it. For what is a man profited, if he shall gain the whole world, and lose his own soul? or what shall a man give in exchange for his soul?

In seeking to be one with the world we seek to distance ourselves from God. The will of God and the will of the sin filled world are diametrically opposed to each other. This goes to another statement Christ made in Matthew 6:24 "No man can serve two masters: for either he will hate the one, and love the other; or else he will hold to the one, and despise the other. Ye cannot serve God and mammon." You cannot serve the sin filled world while at the same time seeking to serve God.

This is why the presence of the Holy Spirit in a believer's life cannot be understated. As mentioned earlier, the Holy Spirit forms the third part of our existence. While the Holy Spirit cannot exist in the presence of the sin nature, that does not mean that it doesn't exist. The Holy Spirit of each unsaved human is held in reserve by God until the time that the individual comes to accept Christ. As Christ described in John 16:13 "howbeit when he, the Spirit of truth, is come, he will guide you into all truth: for he shall not speak of himself; but whatsoever he shall hear, that shall he speak: and he will shew you things to come." In Christ's words we see two very important roles that the Holy Spirit undertakes in the life of a believer. First, the Holy Spirit is the conduit through which we communicate with God. We have already established that God is the source of all truth; therefore, if the Holy Spirit is guiding us in all truth then this must be in communication with God. Secondly, the Holy Spirit acts as a guide in our decision-making process. Prior to an individual accepting Christ, and the Holy Spirit entering their life, a person's decision making is influenced by only two factors: the body and the eternal soul. Under these conditions the world and its sinful influence on the body will almost always win in decisions, thus the reason people do sinful actions before accepting Christ. However, once the Holy Spirit has entered into the life of a believer a third factor begins influencing the decision-making process and the Holy Spirit helps to cast the tie breaking vote in favor of the soul's desire to follow God's will.

The implication here regarding the influence of the Holy Spirit on the decision-making process is earth shattering, because it means that many of the decisions you make before the Holy Spirit enters into your life are void in the eyes of God. Those decisions were on some level sinful, and once the believer accepts Christ's death and resurrection, those sinful decisions are wiped clean in God's sight. This unfortunately does not mean that sinful decisions, made in a sinful world don't still have sinful consequences. The perfect example of this is seen in the earlier discussion of marriage. Two nonbelievers who marry in the eyes of a sinful world are not married in the eyes of God. The action was undertaken through selfish, sinful desires, not the desire to serve God. Furthermore, the decision was made without the input of the Holy Spirit, thus resulting in the decision being made under the influence of sin. Thus, since the decision was not made free from sin and marriage cannot exist within a sinful state, the marriage never really happened from God's perspective.

Jesus illustrates this point very clearly in Matthew 19:8 when He said "He saith unto them, Moses because of the hardness of your hearts suffered you to put away your wives: but from the beginning it was not so." In this passage the "hardness of your hearts" that Christ is referring to is the sin nature. The line "but from the beginning it was not so" is a reference to the fact that God had never intended for marriage to exist in a world filled with sin. If sin had never entered into the world and the Holy Spirit was present in all decisions there would be no need for divorce.

For the individual who accepts that they are in sin, the ultimate destination will always be the Cross of Christ. The Cross represents a very complex aspect of Christianity and can cause confusion for non-believers. For the non-believer they see the cross as a symbol of the Christian faith, the iconic cross on the steeple of a church. However, the struggle we have as followers of Christ is to help non-believers to understand why the Cross was chosen as the symbol for our faith. The Cross symbolizes the completed work that Christ did in redeeming us of our sins. It was in this one definitive act, Christ's sacrifice for all of humanity, that we are able to achieve victory over sin and death. Christ made the decision to give up his life for us, knowing that someone people would never accept him. More than that, Christ knew that as the decades passed that humanity would grow further away from him and begin to ignore his sacrifice.

Our instant culture today is not very inclined towards accepting Christ's finished work because it doesn't occur on a fast-enough timeline. You have to bear the burden of following Christ your entire life before gaining your reward. As Paul said in 2nd Timothy 4:7-8:

> I have fought a good fight, I have finished my course, I have kept the
> faith: Henceforth there is laid up for me a crown of righteousness, which the Lord, the righteous judge, shall give me at that day: and not to me only, but unto all them also that love his appearing.

Following Christ is not easy, and it doesn't get easier with time. The longer you walk this path with Christ, the harder it gets. Society doesn't like people who follow Christ. The life of a person who follows Christ is like a mirror held up to society that highlights ever flaw there is. This is why when we do see a faithful Christian raise to any prominence, society seems to make it a priority to force that person to fall. By making that person fall, their sins don't seem so bad.

You simply cannot come to terms with these realities and not come to the sobering realization that you need Christ in your life. In fact, without Christ you are not truly alive at all as previously mentioned in Paul's comments from Romans 6. Paul's writing in Romans 6 further illustrates the point that we are not truly alive without the indwelling of the Holy Spirit in our lives. Without the Holy Spirit we are incomplete and at risk of eternal death. It's what happened at the Cross that ultimately allows humanity to be freed from the slavery of sin and once again enter into communion with our Creator.   Without Christ's sacrifice at the Cross we are doomed to destruction. We cannot overcome sin by ourselves. We need Christ to overcome sin and the world we have created in sin. It's important to realize the dichotomy that exists here, God created the world and we remade His creation in our own sinful image. Then God sent his Son to die for our sins and ultimately transform the world back into what He originally created.

The Cross is the symbol of the sacrifice and faith that provides our means of salvation it also serves other purposes. The Cross is the hope we have for a better tomorrow and a world free from war, violence and death. The Cross is the ultimate "safe space", it's where we as followers of Christ are free from fear, and any other sinful ideas that lead us to be distant from God's love. The Cross is the symbol of God's unconditional love for all of us. Most people who have grown up in a Christian church know John 3:16 by heart, "For God so loved the world, that he gave his only begotten Son, that whosoever believeth in him should not perish, but have everlasting life.". What is often missed in this passage is the underlying faith that God has in his creation.

God sent His Son to die on the Cross for all of the sins we would ever commit, centuries before we were even born. This faith that God has in humanity to do what is right is a direct result of God being the source of all Truth.

Through the Cross we come to have salvation and peace with God that we cannot achieve any other way. However, our salvation is predicated on faith in Christ's death at the Cross for our sins, which means Christ must have known every sin we would ever commit, otherwise we would be forced to nail Him to the Cross each and every day which is impossible. This is why God's role as the ultimate arbiter of truth is so critical to the faith of any believer.

Chapter 5: A Life Free of Sin?

Can any person live a life completely free from sin? The simple answer is, no. That's what's so miraculous about what Christ did at the Cross. In Christ, the eternal God took on the flesh and blood body of his triune nature to live a life free from sin so that we may have the opportunity to break free from the slavery of sin. When we are born, we don't choose to live in sin. Think of a young child and their dreams of growing up; you don't hear kids say they want to be a drug addict, prostitute or other profession that society looks down upon. Similarly, no person would come into this world making the conscious choice to be enslaved to sin. However, through Christ's sacrifice, we are finally given the choice about how we wish to deal with sin. It took the omnipotence and omnipresence of God to accomplish this task. This is the whole point of God providing the Ten Commandments to Moses in the first place. The standard set by God at Mount Sinai was so high that no human could hope to achieve it without divine intervention. God was seeking to prove to us that the only chance we had for salvation was to accept Christ's finished work at the Cross.

As discussed in an earlier chapter, sin from the view point of humans can be twisted by the perception we see it from. Our perception of sin and our ability to pull away from sin's influence in our lives is directly proportional to the strength of our relationship with God. society makes it difficult to break free from sin. What makes this worse is that so much of the pain and suffering in our lives is the result of sin and exists because of sin. I know that sounds confusing, so allow me to explain. Let's take as an example a person who is terminally ill with cancer. Are they ill because they are in sin? Absolutely not! Are they ill because sin exists in this world? Absolutely! If sin had never entered into the world, there would be no death. God did not create humans to die. We see this in Genesis chapters 2 and 3. There is a lot of emphasis in the Garden of Eden story about Adam and Eve eating from the tree. However, what is often missed is that there were two trees, the Tree of Knowledge and the Tree of Life. God forbid Adam and Eve to eat from the Tree of Knowledge because "…for in the day that you eat of it you shall surely die." God never forbid them from eating of the Tree of Life, thus implying that God had every intention of Adam and Eve living forever. It was the sinful act of eating from the Tree of Knowledge that resulted in humans facing mortality.

The next step in this discussion occurs after the cancer patient has died and how their loved ones react. The stages of grief, as psychologists call it, are fraught with the temptation of sin. Where this is most often seen is in two ways. First, is the individual who blames God. As discussed in Chapter 2, God did not create sin. It is not God's fault that sin exists in the world we live in. And despite what many people seem to believe, Satan didn't create sin. Satan did exploit God's creation of free will within humans to get us to create sin for him. Satan did this intentionally, because the goal is to prove to God that humans are inferior and unworthy of God's unconditional love and grace. It was Adam and Eve who created sin as a direct result of their disobedient actions towards God. Furthermore, from the moment of their disobedience, the world we live in is has not been the world God created. This is the world our sinful ideas created. God's perfect creation is not the world we live in today. In God's perfect creation there was no death, no war, no violence, or any of the other issues that we have created out of our sinful minds.

Second, is the belief that there is some way to

stop sin and death from occurring. Death is a natural consequence of sin. That's why we will never be able to live in this world and be free from sin. The consequence of the sinful nature of humanity will always be present until Christ returns and God's perfect kingdom is reestablished. We can spend all the money we want trying to find a cure for every medical and social condition on the planet. However, even if we found the cure for all of them, something else would replace them. No matter how much we may try, we will never be able to overcome sin on our own.

Another important realization is that sin that what makes something sinful is our knowledge that it's sinful. Once you know something is sinful, it will always be sinful. Once you are aware of the sin in your life, there is no undoing that knowledge. This is important, because the concepts of "right and wrong" and "good and evil" are to a certain extent subjective. While most people grow up being enculturated about what is "right and wrong", those concepts are not universal. Let's take as an example the person who calls you perpetrating a telemarketing scam. To most of us, this kind of activity is clearly unacceptable. However, it's clear that for parts of our society, this is a permissible activity.

This knowledge does not represent an escape clause from God's divine judgement. The subjective nature of "right and wrong" and the result of the way sin twists our perceptions. Just because the concept of "right and wrong" is subjective, does not mean that you can do whatever you want and claim that you don't see it as wrong. Let's use the analogy of a sports car. You can't take a sports car, replace the engine with one from an economy car, and then complain to the manufacture because the car doesn't run correctly. Yet this is exactly what many people do to God. They want to change the rules to fit their beliefs and not God's and then blame God because life turns out wrong. To be brutally clear about this, our lives are created by God, and run according to God's rules. And no matter how much you might want to do so, taking your ball and going home is not an option.

The fact that sin exists in the world, provides you with the realization that something is "wrong", regardless of how that perception is twisted by sin. We again see this play out in the Garden of Eden. Eating of the fruit of the Tree of Knowledge was wrong because God had told them what would happen if they did. However, Adam and Eve did not fully know the consequences of entering into sin until after they had committed the deed. Similarly, Adam and Eve were walking around in the Garden of Eden nude, with no concept that this was embarrassing or morally objectionable. Once they had eaten the fruit, they knew immediately that what actions they had taken that were sinful. We see the result of sin play out in the moment after eating the fruit. First, they covered their nudity. Second, they hide from God. Third, they lied to God. Even in the beginning we see how one sin leads to another, and another as it compounds the problem.

God knew from the beginning that sin was going to enter into the world in the Garden of Eden. Sin was an inevitable byproduct of God's perfect creation. I know that sounds like a contradiction and there are some nonbelievers who will argue that if God knew before creation that sin was going to enter into His perfect creation, then why didn't he just remove the Tree of Knowledge from the Garden of Eden? Why didn't God simply ban Satan from entering the Garden of Eden? Why would an omnipotent God allow these things to happen when he knew it would happen and could have stopped it? The problem is that God's prefect creation included the existence of free will. We have to remember that we are created in God's perfect image and that God's prefect image is a matter of God's perspective. Therefore, if God has free will then humans must have free will also, but it doesn't mean that we are capable of exercising that free will with the same ability God can. Let's face it, free will is undoubtably easier for God to execute in his omnipotent, omniscient and omnipresent state. We also must remember that the concept of God having free will is very important to the existence of salvation through Christ. God's choice to send His Son to die for our sins was a choice made out of free will. Christ himself said that he had the ability to lay his life down for the sins of mankind and to take it up again. Christ made a choice by His own free will to serve as the sin sacrifice for all of humanity. Similarly, we as believers must make the choice by free will to accept Christs finished work on the cross.

This is not to say that our choice is as easy as Christ's was. For us as humans, the choice to accept Christ is made more difficult because of sin. The decision to accept Christ has to be one made of our own free will, despite the influence of sin. It cannot be a decision made under duress or coercion. God does not want His heavenly kingdom to be full of people who really don't want to be there. God has been down that road before with Lucifer and we all know how that ended. The matter of our creation, and the fact that God created a means for us to achieve salvation is a direct result of Lucifer's rebellion in heaven. Clearly Lucifer and his angelic followers had free will also. The difference was that their free will existed in the presence of sin where Adam and Eve's did not. When Lucifer transformed into the serpent and convinced Eve to grab that fruit, he knew what the result would be. Lucifer knew the result of that knowledge when combined with free will would work to destroy humanity, the same way it will ultimately result in his destruction. Furthermore, Lucifer undertook that action with the intent of destroying God's perfect creation as revenge for being thrown out of heaven. This is where the question of God allowing sin to "occur" becomes complicated. God needed Adam and Eve to eat of the forbidden fruit so that the course of events could be set into action that ultimately would lead to the Cross and salvation for those who freely choose to partake in it.

This concept also brings up the idea of people being "chosen" or "predestined" for salvation. I don't know that either of those words are accurate. This concept comes in part from the gospels of Matthew, Luke and John, where the term "chosen" is used by Christ. The term "predestination" appears twice in Paul's letters to the Romans and Ephesians. I get the sense that these words have been used erroneously by translators over the years. Let's look at Romans 8:29 as an example. In the English translation of this passage Paul says "For whom he did foreknow, he also did predestinate to be conformed to the image of his Son, that he might be the firstborn among many brethren." This passage implies that God has determined who will be saved and who will not, from the beginning of the world. This concept makes no sense in the constructs of an omniscient God. If this was God's intention, then God could have easily snapped His fingers and created all the predestined people He wanted in heaven.

However, since Paul was a Jewish scholar, and was writing the Book of Romans as a letter to Jew living in Rome, it might be beneficial to read a translation of Romans 8:29 from Hebrew. When we do that, Romans 8:29 looks like this, "For, from the beginning, God decided that all believers in Him - and He knew full well who would believe in Him - would resemble His Son, so that His Son would be the firstborn among His brothers." This reading conveys an idea completely different from the standard English translation. In the Hebrew, God, in His omnipotent state, being the source of all truth, knows who will and will not accept the free gift of grace offered by His Son at the Cross. However, God doesn't take an active role in making a determination. Instead God leaves the person to come to a determination of their need for salvation through free will.

Free will and predestination are mutually exclusive concepts. We cannot hold to the belief that God extends free will to us while at the same time believing that God predestines if we will accept Christ. If that were the case there would be no need for evangelism of the gospels since God would have already completed the work. Having the knowledge of right and wrong allows a person with free will to make the conscious choice to do what is wrong, even if that decision is influenced by the sin state of a non-believer. The difference is that the decision to do what is wrong is made easier because of the influence of sin in someone who have never accepted Christ. As mentioned in Chapter 4, the Holy Spirit acts as our guide in the decision-making process. When a person does not have the Holy Spirit to aid in the decision-making process, the outcomes tend to be sinful. In many cases the person still knows that the decision is wrong in a general sense, but lacks the understanding from a spiritual sense of why it's wrong.

As a race, humanity has no choice but to live in a world filled with sin. While this is not a choice we have made, it is a consequence of who we are and no matter how much we might like to do so, we cannot escape that reality. Where we do have a choice is in how we deal with the sin in our lives. The choice in this regard is very simple. Option one is that you choose to acknowledge that you live in sin and that you cannot remedy the situation on your own and need the help of Christ. Option two is that you ignore the problem of sin and hope it just goes away. Option one is the only choice that will resolve the problem. Option two is only going to make life miserable until you either decide that option one works better, or you run out of time to choose.

Chapter 6: Sin and Mental Health

The influence of sin in our lives is very easy to distinguish in a lot of cases. Where it becomes more complicated is in cases where we are unsure if a person truly has the capacity to understand the concept of sin and know the difference between "right and wrong". There are two places where this is seen very clearly in society. The first is with children, which most major Christian denominations deal with in some form through the concept of an "age of accountability", that being an age at which a child is believed to know the difference between "right and wrong" and is accountable for the sins they commit. The other aspect of our society where this is much more uncertain is with individuals who society deem to be "mentally ill". Having worked in the mental health field, I can say without reservation that the mental health community has created a lot of problems when it comes to society dealing with the issue of sin. There are a number of different ways these problems manifest, but I want to discuss a few specifically.

First is the issue of the mental health community in general not being very open to issues of faith. Many of the psychiatrists I have dealt with have a clearly define "god complex". This is so bad in some cases that the doctor will over prescribe psychiatric medication in order to force compliance with the desired treatment from their perspective. The doctor is always right, the patient is always wrong and the doctor is allowed to use whatever means necessary, ethical or otherwise, to get their way. In this environment there is simply no room for God, simply because the doctor doesn't want competition. If someone claims they are hearing the voice of God, they are instantly labeled as schizophrenic and started on high doses of anti-psychotic medication.

The notion that a person might actually be having a religious experience is almost never considered. In 1 John 4:1 we are told as believes to "…believe not every spirit, but try the spirits whether they are of God…". If someone tells me that they are being told be a voice claiming to be God to go help the homeless, then I'm inclined to believe that they may be having a genuine spiritual experience. If someone tells me that the voice of God is telling them to murder people, I'm going to be inclined to say something else is going on. The sad truth is that many times the person who is having a genuine spiritual experience is treated worse by the mental health community than the person who is truly psychotic. The reason for this is that the person who is having a religious experience is more likely to resist "treatment" for their "diagnosis" than the person who is truly psychotic. The person who refuses treatment is quickly labeled as "defiant" or "dangerous to themselves". Once we start down that path all kinds of other problems start to evolve; particularly since "religious devotion" is now identified as a psychiatric disorder in the Diagnostic and Statistical Manual of Mental Disorders.

   The next area within the mental health community that is problematic for society involves issues of control and the law. The idea that all mental health professionals are looking to help people in need is completely false. Let me be clear, there is a small group within the mental health community, generally made up of people who have their own mental health diagnosis, who are trying to help. Unfortunately, the majority of people who I have dealt with in positions of authority are only concerned with controlling other people. The manner in which they exert control is largely hidden from the public and is shocking. Let's start with the first instance of someone interacting with the mental health community in a crisis setting. This normally involves the person being taken to an emergency room of a local hospital by the police. It is becoming common place for police departments to have dedicated mental health professionals who are referred to as "co-responders" assist in this process. Once the person is in the emergency room there are a number of medical tests done to rule out an underlying medical condition.

At some point before the person is "medically cleared" they will be interviewed by a qualified mental health professional. This person can be the co-responder or someone from the local community mental health center. This is where the process begins to take a draconian turn. Prior to conducting the interview many of these qualified mental health professionals will request the emergency room physician to administer an injection of Ativan, Xanax, Haldol, or some other drug. To put this in perspective, this like a police officer pulling you over and demanding that you take four shots of whiskey prior to conducting a field sobriety test. If that were the way field sobriety testing was conducted, everyone would end up in jail for DUI. Similarly, a shocking number of people who are screened by the qualified mental health professionals are deemed to be in need of inpatient care because the medications they were given prior to the interview caused them to hallucinate.

Once the person is deemed to be in need of hospitalization, they can either go voluntarily or involuntarily. The situation gets much worse in the case of involuntary commitment. In an involuntary commitment the person is held on a temporary court order for anywhere from three to seven days before they are required to go before a judge. But there is a caveat to this requirement. If the treating psychiatrist informs the judge that the patient's presence at the hearing would be detrimental to their mental health, then the patient is denied their appearance and a court appointed attorney appears in their place. At this point the judge can issue a "care and treatment order" that allows the government to forcibly hospitalize the patient for anywhere from 30 days to six months. To make matters worse, the court appointed attorney has every incentive to keep the patient hospitalized because they will get paid again for the next court appearance. There are attorneys who make their living doing nothing but handling these types of cases. They appear in court, they never raise any objections, they never ask any questions, and they agree to everything the doctor says before signing the treatment order and moving on to the next case. It is possible for a patient to be hospitalized for years without ever seeing a judge. While the mental health and legal communities insist that this charade of a system meets the standards of due process, only a third world dictator would actually believe that.

As if the complete lack of due process wasn't bad enough, there is a disturbingly high number of people who are committed to psychiatric facilities who end up with court appointed guardians. Once again this is done without the patient's consent and often times over the objections of the patient. Shortly after the guardianship is established the patient will find themselves with a "payee" who will take control of their finances. The assignment of the payee only requires the signature of the treating psychiatrist and a witness. What I found truly disturbing was that fact that in some cases the payee becomes the state government. This allows the state government to legally pilfer the bank accounts and other assets of the patients the state's courts are forcing to be held against their will. In the most extreme cases at state run hospitals some of the patients work in "supported employment" positions as state employees, only to have the state use their position as payee to take the money they earn.

   The third area where the mental health community causes problems for dealing with sin in society is with the use of medication. Let's begin by clearing the air on a couple of issues regarding psychiatric medications. First, most of these medications don't actually work. In a 2007 study of data submitted to the FDA during clinical trials of antidepressants found that only 1.3% of patients actually benefited from the medication. In the best-case scenarios, antidepressants are only effect in helping a person achieve long term recovery from depression in less than 25% of cases. Contrast this with treatment modalities that focus on behavioral changes, such as therapeutic lifestyle change, which have a long-term recovery rate of over 75%. These facts make complete sense when viewed from the stand point of a sin filled world. Our sin nature drives us to engage in behavior that is detrimental to out mental wellbeing. Sin drives us to self-isolate, to eat in an unhealthy way, and to avoid exercise. These are all things that have been proven to cause mental health issues.

   The problem with using medication in this area is twofold. First, the medication covers up the symptoms of what sin is doing to the mind. By changing brain chemistry, we are changing the way people behave. Covering up the problem does not make the problem go away. Imagine if you were to develop a leak in the radiator hose of your car while driving down the road. If you're well prepared you have some duct tape in your car and have the ability to patch the leak until you can get someplace and replace the hose. However, if you put the duct tape on the hose and ignore the problem, eventually the adhesive on the duct tape will wear out and the leak will resume. Something very similar happens with psychiatric medications. The medications will work for a time, but as the brain adjusts to the chemical change, the doctor will have to increase the dosage.

The increased dosage leads us to the second problem: side effects. The side effects for many of these drugs are severe to say the least. Lithium can cause toxicity if given for long enough. Clozaril has serious effects on the ability of bone marrow to produce white blood cells. Thorazine causes serious impacts of cognitive function and muscle movements. That's just to name a few of the medications given where the side effects are as bad as the disease. To make matters worse, when these kinds of side effects begin to occur, the patient isn't removed from the medication immediately. These same psychiatrists, with their aforementioned god complex, begin prescribing more medications to cover up the side effects of medications that many times don't actually work. To return to our radiator hose analogy, this is the equivalent of spray painting the duct tape black to match the radiator hose and hoping no one notices. The end result is that these medications are just covering up the problem and not actually solving anything.

To make matters worse over the last decade we are seeing an increasing reliance on the use of psychotropic medication for any number of issues, from depression and anxiety to addiction. However, beyond the chemical side effects that are associated with these medications, there is an unstated psychological side effect that helps to feed sin. In our culture we are raised to believe that when you get sick you take some kind of medication and it helps to make you better. For example, if I have a sinus infection, your doctor will prescribe an antibiotic to help clear the infection up. The cause and effect are clear: there is something wrong with the person so they take a medication to correct whatever is wrong. Our subconscious mind tells us that anytime we're taking a medication, it's because something is wrong with us. Now place this concept in the context of mental health. If you have someone who is the victim of abuse and you give them a psychotropic medication, every time they take that medication it is reinforcing in their mind that they did something wrong. When we do that, we are carving out a niche in their psyche that allows sin to build a fortress that is strengthened with each dose of the medication. It is in this way that these medications are doing untold amounts of damage to people around the world. This is not to say that some people with severe mental disorders do not need medication, but for the vast majority of people suffering for mental health issues, medications are doing much more harm than good.

The sum total of all these problems within the mental health community result in people not getting better. This is really not a surprise however since the same sin that is creating a lot of the mental health issues, we see are also driving the mental health community to exasperate the problem. I would venture to guess that sin is at the root of 95% of the mental health issues I've seen. That doesn't mean that the patient's sinful nature is the cause. However, in many cases it was the sinful actions of someone else that resulted in trauma which brought on a mental health issue. Unfortunately, as a society we have given an incredible amount of power to a very small group of people in the mental health community, and it has not been for our benefit. We have allowed a small group of people, with a very narrow vision of what they perceive to be normal, to define societal norms for the rest of us.

Let's not forget that Christ healed a man living among the tombs of his mental illness. And just like the countless other people Christ healed of various afflictions, the man was told to "go and sin no more". Clearly Christ knew something about dealing with sin and its effect on mental health, and I think this is important to realize when dealing with sin as believers. There seems to be an underlying belief in some parts of Christianity that mental health issues should not exist for believers. I'll be honest, I think menta health issues are probably more prevalent amongst believers in some cases. For the person who doesn't believe, the effects of sin are more powerful, but less noticeable. After all, ignorance is bliss. However, for the believer who is having to live in a world surrounded by sin and deal while trying to live their life for Christ, the burden can be daunting to say the least.

Section Two:
A Sinful Government

Chapter 7: The Government Delusion

As children growing up, we're told in school that our government is tasked with various duties to help the citizens. In the early days of our republic these tasks were fairly minor and designed to aid the nation as a whole. The idea was to allow the 13 original colonies to harness their collective resources for the betterment of all people in the nation. However, as time passed and the boundaries of the United States of America grew, this changed. Today we have a government that struggles to handle even the most basic of tasks, and when the government does succeed in accomplishing a task, it tends to take much longer than needed. The reality is that the government we have is not the government we wanted or the government we need. Unfortunately, the government we need and the government we want is not even close to the same thing. The government we need is one of minimal restriction that forces us to come to terms with who we are as human beings. The government many citizens want today is a "nanny state" that fixes the problems for them. Unfortunately, the government many people want is quite possibly the worst government we could envision in light of the problems we are facing.

Individuality only occurs after someone has accepted Christ as their Savior. Prior to accepting Christ, a person is not making decisions on their own, but their decisions are being guided by their sin nature. Once a person has accepted Christ they are reconnected with God through the Holy Spirit and then that person has the ability to make decisions as an individual. While this might not seem important to the development of government, it is incredibly important in a democracy. Due to a democratic form of government being governed by the decisions of the people, it is imperative that those decisions be made by individuals as opposed to a collective decision that would result in a more communist form of government. This idea extends even further into the issue of human rights. The rights of the individual are at the heart of a representative government. If the individual has no rights, then a representative government is essentially illegitimate.

There are many people reading this book who will instantly say "well the answer is a Godly government". Let me stop you right there. The concept of a "Godly government" is oxymoronic.

God never intended humans to have any governing body except God, because God never intended humans to be "self-governing". The Bible makes it clear that God had no intention of creating government. All things left as they should be, and sin entered the world, there would be no need for government. However, since sin is a major part, if not the controlling influence, of our world, government is necessary to keep society from descending into anarchy.

   In the book of 1ˢᵗ Samuel, we're shown how God views government. Particularly in 1ˢᵗ Samuel 8: 4-7 we read:

> Then all the elders of Israel gathered themselves together, and came to Samuel unto Ramah, and said unto him, "Behold, thou art old, and thy sons walk not in thy ways: now make us a king to judge us like all the nations". But the thing displeased Samuel, when they said, "Give us a king to judge us". And Samuel prayed unto the Lord. And the Lord said unto Samuel, Hearken unto the voice of the people in all that they say unto thee: for they have not rejected thee, but they have rejected me, that I should not reign over them.

What God is telling Samuel in this passage is that the children of Israel want a king because they have been disobedient towards God. Thus, God orders Samuel to give Israel a king, not as a reward, but as a self-fulfilling punishment. In essence, God is telling Samuel to give the Israelites enough rope to hang themselves. Later in 1st Samuel 8 God even goes so far as to instruct Samuel to warn the Israelites of what will happen if they are appointed kings like other nations, and the Israelites refuse to heed God's warning.

When we seek to create governments to hold us accountable, we are subverting the very nature of God. It is God's divine right to judge humanity, not our own right. The strange fact is that our forefathers started to get this correct. They realized that the European monarchies were wrong in their belief that they had a divine right to rule over people. But as is always the case, the sin of pride leads people to believe that they are capable of handling the issues of government themselves. The concept of government serves to illustrate the destructive nature of sin. The only reason we seek government is because we are in sin and yet the government must exist because sin exists. Our concept of government exists because of a logical fallacy created by our own sin nature. Instead of accepting our sinful nature and seeking justification through Christ, we seek to create governments to hold us accountable.

The humans drive to create government a direct response to our sin nature. We innately know that we need to be held accountable for our actions but we are unable to do so, thus we seek to have others do so. Isn't this exactly the role God is supposed to play? Yes, it is. To make matters worse we seem to gravitate towards the extreme ends of forming governments. On the one hand we have people who are completely comfortable with their own sins and the desire no government at all, known as anarchy. On the other hand, we have people who don't want to admit their sins exist, but know that it's there and these people want some form of totalitarian government, be it monarchy, theocracy, or even …democracy!

Yes, democracy is an example of government being used to counter humanity's sin nature. In fact, it might well be the best example of what happens when sinful people try to fix the problem of sin themselves. A group of people get together and decide they can execute government better by having a lot of voices instead of one tyrant dictating how things are done. The whole idea here is that "freedom" is going to make everything better. Unfortunately, "freedom" in the form of free will is what got humans into the whole sin predicament in the first place. As I mentioned in the introduction, freedom comes with a good and bad side, because the same freedom that gives humans the ability to do good also provides the opportunity to do evil.

The point is this: all government is bad and a lack of government is equally bad. All governments end up following the same path of destruction. Things start off great at first, and everyone is happy with the government. However, slowly the government starts to become corrupt because the people making decisions based on the influence of their sin nature. The corruption results in the people become dismissive of the government and demand change. The change normally involves violence, either internal in the form of a revolution or external in the form of conquest. This violence results in a new group taking over control and the cycle starts all over again. As these cycles continue to progress over time the amount of sin continues to build up. Eventually we will be left with a society that will turn on itself simply out of a desire to rid itself of the sin it has created by trying to establish control.

Our founding fathers never intended the constitution we have in place today to last this long. Our founding fathers never intended the constitution to be used to govern a nation of over 330 million people, in fifty states, over seven time zones and stretching across the entire continent. They created the idea of a constitutional convention so that the nation could grow and change. When our nation was founded, it was something that had never been done before and was very much the result of a trial and error approach. The U.S. constitution was never a perfect document and there were cracks from day one. Unfortunately, those cracks have grown over the years into gaping chasms, and in the case of the Ninth and Tenth Amendments a chasm as big as the Grand Canyon.

Truth be known, I believe we're already seeing society turning against itself. The lynch mob mentality we observed during Justice Kavanaugh's confirmation hearings provided a mountain of proof for this occurring. Every precept of justice that our society has developed over the years was systematically destroyed in the vain attempt to keep a conservative voice off the high court. As our sinful pride and desire for power overcome us, we tend to do whatever it takes to prevent ourselves from feeling bad about our sins. For all of the consternation from the far left about abortion and the right to choose, the very idea of abortion is in reality about avoiding the feelings and consequences that come from sin.

God always fulfills his promises to us, that much we can be assured of. God's promises might not always be fulfilled in the timing that we want or in the way that we want, but we can be guaranteed that God will always come through. Unfortunately, the same cannot be said for our government. We've grown accustom to seeing politicians making campaign promises that they can never fulfill and to our government covering up misdeeds so bureaucrats can protect their jobs. However, both of those issues are simply the natural extension of the impact of sin on government. Governments are created based on promises they can never keep.

In my first book *Null and Void* I discussed the concept that the U.S. Constitution was a contract between the citizens of the United States and the government we created for our nation. My argument was that the conditions of that contract, as assigned in the preamble, had been violated by the government, which placed the government in breach of contract. The truth of the matter is that our government entered into a contract it was never capable of fulfilling.   No matter what our government does, it will never be able to provide any of the promises enumerated in the Constitution because our government lacks the divine ability to do so. The government is incapable of providing what is needed by humanity to overcome sin. Yet, we continue to look to government instead of God to fulfill this need.

When we create government and focus on government, we are creating one more space for sin to reign in our lives. In Romans 12:2 Paul wrote "And be not conformed to this world: but be ye transformed by the renewing of your mind, that ye may prove what is that good, and acceptable, and perfect, will of God." If we focus on the world, we will inevitably become sinful like the world we are in. our government and society are a direct representation of the world we have created as a result of sin. We are foolish if we expect the sinful people who have created a sin filled world to correct the problem of sin.

Put very simply, our government is not about justice or preserving the rights of citizens. If all you're willing to do is take a very superficial view of our system of government, then the government we have appears to function properly. However, if you take a moment to pull back the curtain you would see a corrupt judiciary that casts aside citizens' rights and needs like day old bread.

This is the entire problem with the far left and the liberal ideology, that it seeks to mitigate the realities of sin. In my last book, *Governance by Addiction*, I discussed the idea that liberalism is an ideology founded in addict thinking. However, the anxiety people feel towards their own sins is the driving force behind that addict thought process. The hardwiring for addiction is present in every human brain as a result of sin. Addiction is the result of the mind seeking to escape from a painful situation, be it emotional or physical. At its heart, Liberalism is a political theory which seeks to utilize addict thought processes to exploit the anxiety people feel towards sin, and is very effective at doing so.

Chapter 8: *"…establish Justice…"* Revisited

When I originally wrote about the topic of justice in *Null and Void,* I focused on the concept of equality for all citizens. I still think the concept of equal treatment under the law is at the heart of this issue. As Thomas Jefferson wrote, "[t]he true foundation of republican government is the equal right of every citizen; in his person and property, and in their management." Furthermore, we are reminded of Jefferson's immortal words from the Declaration of Independence, "we hold these truths to be self-evident, that all men are created equal…". The problem is that life isn't equal by any stretch of the imagination. If life were equal then people who work hard and put forth the effort to succeed would do so. I grew up with a learning disability and by the time I graduated high school I was reading at a third-grade level. I was told by teachers in school that I would never be able to achieve my dreams because of my disability. However, I trusted in God more than my teachers. After I graduated, I asked God to help me learn to read, and I eventually did teach myself to read well enough to earn two college degrees, without any special accommodations for my disability.

You might think that this is where the story has a happy ending, but you would be wrong. Despite all of my struggles, determination and hard work, I still can't get a job that requires any education above a GED. Is that fair? No. I've put in the work, I've shown myself able to do the job, but I don't even get an interview. Yet, someone who is less qualified gets the opportunity that I have earned. I'll provide an example of this. Shortly after I graduated for the University of Kansas, I applied for a position with a local city government as a geographic information systems (GIS) technician. Now I trained in GIS in college and have a degree in public administration, so it would seem that I would at least get an interview. Not only did I not get an interview, but I later found out, the young woman who got the position had no GIS training, had an associate's degree from the local community college as a pastry chef and only got hired because her mother knew the director of human resources with the city.

The fact of the matter is this, our government cannot legislate or regulate morality and this is at the core of the concept of establishing justice.

Our government has tried with limited success, but overall, the concept of equality and fairness continues to be elusive for most citizens and ideally it shouldn't be this way. When I wrote in *Null and Void* that the "American Dream" had become a pipe dream for many citizens I was correct, and the problems has only gotten worse in the last eight years. While family incomes have gone up a little bit, the cost of health care, child care, and other expenses have increased much more. All of this does nothing more than lead to degradation of the family and the ever-increasing prevalence of divorce, infidelity and domestic violence in our nation.

Our nation is still facing the same problems with lobbyists undermining the will of the voters. Corporate bailouts are common place while the citizens are left unprotected from corporations who engage in negligent activity. There was a time when if a hospital was negligent in their treatment of a patient, the patient would file suit for malpractice and be justly compensated. Now, the patient's medical insurance company would get the money because they had lobbyists convince Congress to pass a law allowing them "first right to recovery" and the patient is left to find their own money to pay for ongoing treatment. That is not justice, that patient has not been made whole in any sense of the term.

We're still allowing the use of arbitrary credit scores when determining if a person should be employed. We have a society that forces people to live in increasing amounts of debt, and yet we continue to hold those same citizens back because of their credit score. The only way these citizens have any hope of getting out from under the debt is to get a better paying job, which is unjustly out of their reach because of their debt. This is a vicious circle created by the banking industry to keep individuals indebted to them. Don't get me wrong, I'm not saying that banks don't have a purpose and that people are not responsible for their actions and decisions when it comes to spending money. What I am saying is that utilizing a completely arbitrary number like a credit score, that has nothing to do with the ability or quality of work an individual can perform, as a metric to make hiring decisions on is absolutely wrong. Furthermore, it boggles my mind that lawyers can figure out a way to file suit against fast food restaurants over the temperature of coffee, but can't figure out a way to abolish the use of credit scores in the hiring process.

In looking back on what I wrote about the concept of establishing justice in *Null and Void* eight years ago, it becomes apparent that our nation continues to fail in this area…and it's not surprising. Simply put, life is not fair because God didn't make life fair for a reason. In recent years we have seen the perceived imbalances in our judicial system result in riots and socials upheaval. One of the more iconic statements to come out of these protests is "No Justice, No Peace". The meaning of this saying has been interpreted several ways. For some it means the continued disruption of the peaceful lives of individuals until the desired form of justice is achieved. For others this saying means that peace cannot exist within their communities without the application of justice. As a follower of Jesus Christ, I know both of these sentiments are wrong. In Romans 5:1 Paul wrote "Therefore being justified by faith, we have peace with God through our Lord Jesus Christ…". If Paul were with us today, I have no doubt that he would tell protestors that is they know justification, then they will know peace.

In referencing the King James Bible, the word "justice" appears 28 times in The Old Testament. In all but six occurrences the word "justice" is used alongside the term "judgment". The two words are used together because the concepts are connected. In a legal sense, justice means to be made whole. The goal of justice is to return a person or group of people to the condition they were in prior to an injustice being rendered against them. In order to rectify the injustice, the individual or group responsible for the establishment of justice must pass judgment in deciding if an injustice occurred. For example, when a criminal is put on trial, the courts make a judgment about the guilt or innocence of the defendant. If found guilty, the defendant is sentenced to be punished for their crime and justice is perceived to have been done.

However, in turning to the King James Bible again, we notice the word "justice" never appears in The New Testament. A closer examination reveals the word "justice" has been replaced with the word "justified", which appears 27 times in The New Testament. The term "justified" means justice has been accomplished, and the injured parties have been made whole. The term justified is the natural extension of the penultimate event of The New Testament, the crucifixion and resurrection of Jesus Christ. In giving his life on the cross, Christ served as the ultimate sacrifice for the sins of humanity. As a result of His sacrifice, we as believers have been made whole and returned to God's grace. It is the result of our faith in the redemptive power of Christ's sacrifice on the cross by which we have been justified.

The human concept of justice is nothing more than an illusion; a veil pulled over our eyes by our sin nature through which we see a monochromatic world of right and wrong. When our courts hand out justice, it rarely makes anyone whole. If a homicide is committed and the killer is executed, does the victim regain their life? When a police officer writes a speeding citation, who was the injustice done against and who is made whole when the fine is paid? Our government and legal system exist because of the innate desire of one human being to harm another. If it were not for sin, we would have no need for laws and the law will never be a solution to the problem of sin. As Paul wrote in Romans 3:19-20:

> Now we know that what things soever the law saith, it saith to them who are under the law: that every mouth may be stopped, and all the world may become guilty before God. Therefore by the deeds of the law there shall no flesh be justified in his sight: for by the law is the knowledge of sin.

In the simplest terms, our sense of justice is the result of our flawed desire to reconcile the sin nature while attempting to ignore that we need God in our lives. As humans we're not equipped with the ability to correct our sinful ways without Christ.

The only true sense of justice for all of humanity is the justification which comes from accepting Christ and repenting of our sins. Logic dictates that in order to know justice we must first recognize the justification Christ secured for us at the Cross. Just as the knowledge of justice requires acceptance of Christ, the knowledge of peace requires us to first be justified. In John 14:27 we're told that Jesus said "Peace I leave with you, my peace I give unto you: not as the world giveth, give I unto you. Let not your heart be troubled, neither let it be afraid." Upon recognizing the illusionary nature of the world's form of justice, we can also come to realize the illusionary nature of the world's peace when contrasted with the eternal peace offered by Christ. A person can never know peace as long as they are at war with their own sins. Only through justification can we be freed from the bondage of sin and thus know the true peace offered by God.

Unfortunately, instead of seeking spiritual justification through Christ, we often go in search of the illusion of justice offered by humanity. It should come as no surprise when the illusion of justice fails to bring us peace. After all illusionary justice does nothing to free us from being slaves to sin. To make matters worse, the further we chase after the illusion of justice the further we find ourselves removed from God. We're told in Matthew 6:14-15 that Jesus said "For if ye forgive men their trespasses, your heavenly Father will also forgive you: But if ye forgive not men their trespasses, neither will your Father forgive your trespasses." I have never seen a person who is seeking their own concept of justice and has also forgiven the people who have committed a perceived injustice against them. God's solution for attaining justice was to forgive the sins of humanity so we could be made whole. The government is incapable of providing what is needed by humanity to attain justice because of sin. Yet, we continue to look to the government instead of God to fulfill this need.

There is no government in the world that will be capable of establishing justice as was promises in the preamble of the U.S. Constitution. Only God is capable of establishing justice for humanity. Furthermore, God has already established the only justice that matters when he sent his son to die for our sins. While the injustices that we deal with in life might seem like major issues, in the cosmic scheme of things, it's a minor bump in the road. In 1st Corinthians 6:1-2 Paul commented on this concept when he said:

>   Dare any of you, having a matter

against another, go to law before the unjust, and not before the saints? Do ye not know that the saints shall judge the world? and if the world shall be judged by you, are ye unworthy to judge the smallest matters?

We can see from Paul's writing to the believers in Corinth that believers should not be seeking after the false justice of the world, but after the justification of God. Notice also that Paul says the world will be judged by the saints, but the saints will not be judging those of us who know Christ. Clearly there would be no need to judge those of us who have already been justified through the blood of Christ. This judgement if reserved for those who refuse to accept Christ and elect to follow after sin.

When it comes to justice, there is no hope for sinful humans to ever establish any system that will provide justice to everyone. We live in a sinful world and there are always going to be winners and losers. This can't be helped as it's just part of the impact that sin has on us. The only thing we can control is how we treat others. If you wish to have justice then do two things. First, come to know Jesus Christ as your personal lord and savior and thereby have justification with God. Secondly, follow the teachings of Christ and love your neighbors, do

go to those who hate you and persecute you. If
you complete these two tasks, you are
guaranteed to find a form of eternal justice that
man can never create.

Chapter 9:
"*…insure domestic Tranquility…*" Revisited

When I wrote the second chapter of *Null and Void*, I opened with a discussion about the United States in the post 9/11 world and wrote the following:

> When over three dozen electronic devices can be planted around a major metropolitan area such as Boston and no one notices, it greatly troubles me. What if those had been explosive devices planted by terrorist, instead of being part of a stupid advertising campaign gone horribly awry? If it had been a terrorist attack the hangers at Logan International would have been used as temporary morgues.

I really wish that the city officials in Boston had read that prior to the marathon bombing.

Clearly, we haven't had another terrorist attack on the same level as 9/11 in the eight years since I wrote *Null and Void*, but that doesn't necessarily mean we are any safer.

Looking back on chapter two of *Null and Void* I begin to see some of the early ideas that created the foundation of this book. I'm particularly drawn to a quote I used from
Thomas Paine and I think it's just as fitting to use it again here:

> For were the impulses of conscience clear, uniform, and irresistibly obeyed, man would need no other lawgiver; but that not being the case, he finds it necessary to surrender up a part of his property to furnish means for the protection of the rest; and this he is induced to do by the same prudence which in every other case advises him out of two evils to choose the least. Wherefore, security being the true design and end of government, it unanswerably follows that whatever form thereof appears most likely to ensure it to us, with the least expense and greatest benefit, is preferable to all others.

The truth is that we need government because there are sinful people in the world who wish to harm us. As a result, we seek other sinful people to take charge of protecting us. And inevitably, those sinful people engage in sinful actions that put us in ever greater danger of being harmed by other sinful people, and the vicious cycle continues. Simply stated, all governments are the result of a sinful reaction, to sinful people, doing sinful things.

There has never been a government created capable of ensuring domestic tranquility, outside of God and there never will be one. Peace does not come from the law, the only thing you will receive from the law is pain and death. The problem is that we as a society have tried to replace true peace with the concept of freedom. We've come to believe that having peace means that we are free to do what we want, but this simply isn't true. We defend our freedoms with great zeal, and we vote based on the way others perceive our freedoms. The uncomfortable truth is that our freedoms are an illusion created in our own minds for the purpose of justifying our sin nature. We tend to see freedoms as a default setting on our moral compasses. Sin causes us to erroneously believe that when we have the freedom to do something it must be good. If I'm over 21 years old, I have the freedom to drink alcohol, and smoke tobacco, and do a lot of other things. However, just because I have the freedom to engage in those activities does not mean that doing so is good for me as a person or for society as a whole.

This is where the true spiritual pitfalls of democracy and representative government are most visible. When inherently sinful people create sinful laws in a sinful world, the end result will always be sin. Even if you think the law is meant to do good, it will inevitably be twisted by humans into some form of sinful behavior. A perfect example of this would be prohibitions on abortion.

Let me be clear before I start, I think abortion as a form of birth control is an absolutely horrible act that should never occur and is the culmination of a whole lot of sinful behavior. However, banning abortion would simply have the effect of forcing it underground and cause a lot of women to dying due to botched procedures. The end result would be society seeking to relegalize abortion to prevent those deaths, thus making the end result even worse than where we began. To make matters worse, the sin nature is the driving force behind both sides of that argument. The pro-abortion faction is being driven by their desire to make sinful choices without consequences. The pro-life faction is being driven by the desire to condemn those who are making sinful decisions, which Christ said not to do.

As a society we cannot regulate, litigate or legislate morality. I'm reminded of a line from Paul in 1st Corinthians 8:9, "But take heed lest by any means this liberty of yours become a stumbling block to them that are weak." It is not laws that regulate freedom, but our own actions. It is not the law that gives us peace, but our relationship with Christ. If we desire to take actions that harm others for our own benefit, then we continue in sin. This goes back to the concept mentioned in Chapter 4 about sin being rooted in selfishness. We say that we want our government to "ensure domestic tranquility", but then we utilize the freedoms that same government has given us to undermine our relationship with God, and jeopardizing our sense of true peace. The government cannot force you to find peace with God. The government can spend billions in tax dollars every year fighting terrorists, providing economic security and addressing any other of a myriad of social issues, and it won't give you lasting peace. There will still be sin in the world, there will still be people who want to do you harm.

To make matters worse, in the eight years since I wrote *Null and Void*, our society has moved further away from God and more towards sin in many areas. As a result, Christians are facing an increasing amount of persecution in the United States today. In chapter two of *Null and Void* I quoted Paul in Romans 13 saying "For rulers are not a terror to good works, but to evil. Do you want to be unafraid of the authority? Do what is good, and you will have praise from the same." The current state of affairs in the United States is the opposite of what Paul described.

More and more we are seeing the government and the law used as a weapon against the political opponents of the far-left. The framers of the Constitution feared that the law could be weaponized and as a result included the Fifth Amendment's protects for those facing criminal prosecution. The right to protection from self-incrimination is a very important right and one that all citizens should be able to trust in their ability to apply. Unfortunately, most citizens would be hard pressed to know when they can actually exert this protection without a lengthy discussion with legal counsel. No right extended to the people by the government should ever be that complicated.

Most troubling of all is how the far left has sought to utilize the confusion surrounding the "right to remain silent" to mask their efforts to weaponize this aspect of the Fifth Amendment. The best example we can see for this is the fraudulent case against former National Security Advisor Michael Flynn. Former FBI director James Comey admitted in testimony before the

U.S. House of Representatives in December of 2018 the following:

> I'd never worked in a transition time before, but my understanding was that, in a more established administrative environment, you wouldn't get away with just calling the witness and saying, 'Can we come and talk to you?'

Let's be very clear about what happened here. James Comey sent two FBI agents, one of whom had a known political bias, to the White House to question Michael Flynn when Comey viewed Flynn as a suspect in an ongoing criminal investigation. James Comey did this intentionally during a period of time when he knew he could get away with violating standard protocol and that it was unlikely that White House legal counsel would have been present. The agents then questioned Michael Flynn without informing him that lying to them would constitute a criminal offense, and presumably without advising him of his Miranda Rights as well. Even if Michael Flynn had been advised of his Miranda Rights, he likely would have refused access to counsel. We know this because former FBI Deputy Director Andrew McCabe admitted in a memo to making a coercive statement to Michael Flynn threatening to involve the U.S. Department of Justice if Flynn were to request counsel.

Based on the outcome of this series of events, the FBI charged Michael Flynn. However, the charge was not related to the original criminal investigation, but for lying to the FBI during a course of question that probably never should have occurred. To make the matter even worse, since Michael Flynn was not charged with a crime arising from the original investigation, we can't help but wonder if the FBI even possessed adequate probable cause to have been questioning Flynn in the first place. The actions of James Comey and the FBI officials involved in this incident was clearly unethical, and while it might not be called "illegal" it definitely exists in a grey area of the law.

What does this mean for the rest of us? If a cabinet level member of a presidential administration can be treated in this fashion by law enforcement, then what hope is there for the rest of us? What if we see another IRS targeting scandal, but next time the IRS calls conservatives in for audits and tries to deny them access to legal counsel? The self-incrimination protection found in the Fifth Amendment has already become difficult to enforce in IRS related matters. Where exactly do we draw the line on this issue? How can we hope to have any form of domestic tranquility when a political party is allowed to apply biased opinions to legal matters to fulfill their own political objectives?

Another area where we have seen this issue come to light over recent years was in the law suits filed against bakeries for refusing to create a cake for homosexual weddings. Let's be clear on this point, it is the prerogative of a private business owner to decide who they wish to do business with. This goes for any private business, from a bakery to a hospital. It is the business that is putting its name and reputation on the line when they conduct business with someone. Unfortunately, the far left looks to apply our laws in a selective manner in many cases. Someone should not be forced to undertake a task that they are uncomfortable with. Is this to say that a doctor who is unsure of their ability to perform a complicated surgery can be forced to perform the surgery? Is it fair to force that doctor to assume the risk and other liabilities associated with that task?

While I understand that there is a certain segment of our population that is offended by the political positions of various businesses, that does not give you the right to force your will upon them. We function in a capitalist economic system, if you don't like how a company does business, then take your business elsewhere. If enough people disapprove of their business practices, then their business will fail. It is not the job of government to legislate morality based on what one particular group believes. Once again this is a matter of selective application by liberals. The far left seems to have no problem with financial institutions refusing to provide services to firearms related businesses, despite the fact that the right to keep and bear arms is constitutionally protected.

The genesis of this problem is sin. As discussed earlier in this book, the concept of individuality is a very Christian concept. Individuality is a requirement of Christianity because an individual must take responsibility for their sins in order to accept Christ. This is the reason liberals are so determined to attack individuality at any opportunity. Part of our efforts to combat sin in our nation has to include promoting individuality and personal responsibility. While the left likes to claim that they promote individuality through "inclusion", this is absolutely not true. Liberals are only willing to be inclusive of ideas they support, or more accurately, ideas that support their sinful goals.

The reason the left utilizes the law to attack individuality is because it they want to banish

individuality and the accountability that it involves. To the far left the idea of an individual protection from self-incrimination seems to be an archaic "negative right". Liberals would prefer to do away with protections from self-incrimination in favor of a government duty to ensure justice at all costs. According to the twist sense of justice held by liberals, the goal is to replace "negative rights" the promote individual liberty with "positive rights" that seek to provide protects to entire classes of people. According to the liberal view, "positive rights" provide for universal justice that allows more equality to select classes of people who they define. The problem is that this concept of "positive rights" is nothing more than a sinful justification for attacking individuality and promoting more sinful beliefs. From the stand point of justice this concept represents an
incredibly dangerous and misguided view of the law.

We live in a very challenging time. I would venture to say that never in the history of humanity have we seen a world with so much potential to both recreate itself and destroy itself at the same time. Unfortunately, the nature of sin dictates that we as a human race are much more likely to choose destruction over creation. To make matters worse, most of the people in our government, and the rest of the world for that matter, allow sin to be the driving force on their decision making. Sin is not known for creating peace and tranquility. Domestic tranquility must start with God. A sinful government run by sinful people will never be able to provide peace of mind to anyone. Looking to the government or the law for peace of mind will only lead to frustration. However, God can provide a sense of peace that is eternal.

Chapter 10:
"*...provide for the common Defense...*" Revisited

When I wrote *Null and Void* and discussed this section of the preamble, I focused a lot on the military nature of the United States. While I stand behind what I said eight years prior, I think in revisiting the issue of "common defense" it is important to look at how the sin nature plays into our nation's propensity to enter into military conflict and some of the misguided doctrines that have resulted.

When I originally wrote on this topic, I made the point that warfare is inevitable, and that is absolutely true. The inevitability of war and conflict in general is a natural result of our sin nature. Sin breeds conflict so it is only natural that a sinful world with sinful humans would be subject to sinful actions that result in conflict and violence. Sin does not lend itself to rationality and civil discourse. In all of the decades I've spent studying the history of wars I've yet to discover a war that resulted from good intentions. Wars tend to be the result of greed and hatred. It is not the natural inclination for people to want to kill other people without a perceived cause. There is always some issue that others have perceived as being a justification for fighting a war.

This concept of perception and justification brings us to one of the overriding issues that I failed to address in *Null and Void* when discussing this topic. As Christians we have been brought up with the concept known as "just war theory", which means we believe that there are conditions under which it is acceptable to go to war and kill other human beings. The problem with just war theory is that it normalizes warfare, it makes warfare seem like a purely intellectual debate as opposed to a spiritual issue. Particularly with regards to St. Aquinas' view of just war, the decision to fight a war is boiled down to nothing more than some simple yes and no criteria to be addressed, and if the proper answers are provided then there is a sense of support from God for the conduct of a war. The uncomfortable truth is that we can take the belligerents of any conflict and apply just war theory to the events from their perspective and create a justification for the war to be fought.

This is not to say that there is never a justified reason to fight a war, but that the ethical test we use in Christianity for determining this is very flawed. We don't always realize it, but just war theory is myopic in that it only focuses on the perception of one party in the conflict. As a result, any conflict that derives its justification solely from just war theory is suspect of being unjust in reality. In very few cases is an offensive war ever going to be justified for three primary reasons. First, any offensive war without any sign of aggression from the party being attacked is never justified anyway. Secondly, even if there are indications that the other side is preparing an attack and the war is justified as a preemptive strike, the nature of sin will always cloud our judgement and make us see things that aren't there. Third, the nature of sin is the driving force behind aggression, so any military action a nation takes will always have an undercurrent of sinfulness involved. This is why we have rarely seen problems solved long term through the use of warfare. We have seen all three of these realities play out in our nation's own military history.

While many foreign policy initiatives proposed by the Democratic Party have resulted in disastrous wars for our nation, the Truman Doctrine probably did more damage than any other. The Truman Doctrine also provides us with two prime examples of an offensive wars in which the United States was not under attack. While the conflicts in both Korea and Vietnam provide good examples, I think the Vietnam War is a much better example due to the way it began. The Johnson administration knew that they lacked a justification to take the United States into a war in Vietnam. As a result, the Johnson administration concocted a phony attack in the Gulf of Tonkin to meet the standard of just war theory. From the perspective of many U.S. citizens the only truth they knew was of the events came from the news media. At that time citizens had no other means of getting the truth about events and the media was notorious for covering up events that took place in government. While we would hope that a similar event would not occur today due to the prevalence of independent media and the internet, there are some disturbing trends that have surfaced that raise concerns about what the future holds.

In recent years we have seen a sharp rise in the targeting of conservative voices in the various spheres of social media. The argument that many liberals make is that social media platforms are private entities and have the right to define who has access to their services and what type of content can be published. To be honest I think there is a fundamental problem with that line of thought. A nation cannot continue to be free as long as the ability to freely express ideas is suppressed. This concept is at the core of the first Amendment's protections on freedom of speech. Yet for liberals the notion of the free exchange of any idea that contradicts their own is unacceptable. The reason for this is surprisingly simple. Most of the ideas expressed by the far left lack any logical defense. For the left to allow logic and reason to guide the direction of political discourse in our society would result in them losing virtually every argument. This leaves the left with no other option but to seek opportunities to ban any speech that highlights the truth or challenges the narrative they wish to present.

As a result of these issues, many social media sites are coming under increased scrutiny for their censoring of free speech and independent press. Looking at the history of the Democratic Party, we can clearly see that the trajectory we are currently on is leading us in the direction of a social media version of Jim Crow, where conservative voices of reason with the ability to make cognitive impacts, are segregated into the obscure corners of the internet. What is truly concerning about the pending segregation is the method in which liberals rationalize it. I've come across many on the far left who believe the social media service providers are within their rights as private businesses to ban whomever they wish. The problem with this line of thinking is that those same social media providers are allowing government agencies to function on their networks. The First Amendment gives "We the People…" the right "…to petition the Government for a redress of grievances." As a result, we as citizens are legally entitled to exercise our First Amendment rights to freedom of the press, speech and assembly in any sphere where the government operates. Social media providers have made the choice to open their doors to the U.S. Government, and as a result they should be legally obligated to extend First Amendment, and any other applicable Constitutional protections, to the U.S. citizens who utilize their services also.

The far left's ideas regarding social media censorship also has some other chilling consequences that many have not realized. If our rights as citizens do not extend to private networks, then what is to stop government agencies from moving their files to those networks and using it as a shield to protect them from requests under the Freedom of Information Act? In fact, I would argue that the ideas the far left is using to rationalize social media censorship is just a natural extension of the rationalization Hillary Clinton used when she established a private email server.

The First Amendment is directly tied tour our nation's ability to "provide for the common defense", because it allows citizens to hold the government accountable when they involve our nation in wars based on truly unjustifiable causes. Without sufficient knowledge of the cause for a war we are left at the mercy of a sinful government that could be acting in a way that is not consistent with the will of the people. To make matters worse, the nature of sin will drive people to agree to a war out of fear of what might happen. Sin is very good at playing on the fears of people, and can cause our minds to justify some truly horrific things is we allow it to.

The second situation where an offensive war is not justified is when sin has clouded our perspective of reality. The best example of this is seen during the Second Iraq War. While many liberals believe that this war was unjust simply because it was a war of greed, the facts simply don't show that to be true. To understand what happened with the events that resulted in both the Second Iraq War and the terrorist attacks of 9/11 we have to look to the events that occurred in the later years of the Clinton Administration. In 1998 the Clinton administration presented Congress with a budget that resulted in a surplus, which in turn resulted in checks being sent to all U.S. taxpayers. The way that the Clinton administration achieved this surplus was by cutting funding to areas of the government the Democratic Party saw as less important. These areas included the government's defense and intelligence functions. This action had two major impacts on the defensive capability of the United States in the time period leading up to and following the 9/11 attacks. First, the NSA was left so underfunded by the Clinton administration that they were unable to review the previous weekend telephone intercept from Osama Bin Laden warning his mother of the 9/11 attacks until almost 12 hours after the attacks took place. Secondly, it left our intelligence ability so decimated that it forced the Bush administration to adopt procedures that resulted in less than reliable intelligence from disreputable sources. The result was be intelligence that lead to a war in Iraq that should have never occurred.

The perceived threat to the nation made our government susceptible to the sin's ability to twist our perception of the truth. We were forced to rely on intelligence from sources that our government would normally have avoided. We were forced to take actions under the belief that failure to do so could result in another attack and further loss of life. All of this is an example of how sin plays on our sense of fear during unpredictable times. When we let our feelings of fear run wild, we allow sin to creep into our minds and cloud our perspective. We have to remember that sin feeds on fear mor than any other emotion. From the stand point of the Bush administration they had every reason to believe that the information they had received was correct. Within the confines of bounded rationality, they had all of the information that would be available to them at the time and made a decision based on that information. Now I'm sure that many on the far left will claim that they should have sought more information or listened to liberal voices, but let's not forget that many Democrats voted to go to war in Iraq also. Some were even so brazen as to claim that they voted for the war before they voted against the war.

Ideally our government would never be put in the position of have to make what are viewed as life and death decision with limited information. However, these kinds of decisions are made by our government every day, but most of them are unreported by the media. Prosecutors make choices about who to charge with a crime. If they charge the person and there isn't enough evidence, the suspect might not be convicted. If they fail to charge the person they might go out and victimize someone else while waiting for more evidence to be found. If they charge an innocent person too soon, they may not discover the error until after damage has been done to an innocent person's reputation. This is but one example of the hard choices our government must make every day. It also illustrates the reason why we need individuals in our government who are making wise decisions with minimal interference from sin.

The third situation where our sin nature is serving as the driving force behind our actions. The best example of this is seen in the War in Afghanistan. In the rush to avenge the deaths of U.S. citizens, we attacked a nation whose involvement with the events of 9/11 was actually rather minor. The people of Afghanistan saw their nation torn apart because the warlords in control allowed Bin Laden safe harbor in a mountain cave in Tora Bora. By comparison, Pakistan allowed Bin Laden to live in a three-story compound in a major city and suffered no consequences. In fact, the U.S. taxpayers continued to provide aid to the government of Pakistan for six years after Bin Laden was killed in their nation.

Sin does some of its most powerful work when

we are seeking revenge for a wrong that has been done to us. In those situations, sin will drive us to do things we normally wouldn't do. It will drive us to lie, to cheat, and even to break laws. Sin has the powerful ability to allow us to justify actions that we know are wrong. While this happens with warfare, it also happens in society as a whole. Ever since President Trump was elected, we have seen a rise in the number of people hoaxing hate crimes and other events to create a false sense of sympathy for their political agenda. The goal in these cases is to create a condition where people will act out of their sinful desire for revenge as opposed to allowing reason and logic to guide their actions. This concept is at the root of the identity politics that are playing out in our nation today. Virtually all false political narratives focus on an "us against them" platform.

This is not to say that all wars fought out of "revenge" are unjust or influenced by sin. I think the perfect example of this is the U.S. response to the attack on Pearl Harbor at the beginning of World War II. Following the attack, the U.S. did not launch a full retaliatory strike against the imperial Japanese immediately. Instead our government took the time to step back and collect itself before taking action. It was six month later before the U.S. naval forces engaged the Japanese at the Battle of the Coral Sea and seven months before the Battle of Midway. This time allowed the U.S. military to position forces and study enemy movements before any battle. This lack of a significant response also resulted in the Japanese forces becoming overconfident in their abilities. Consequently, the Japanese over committed in the Coral Sea and the U.S. was successful in blunting their imperial expansion. By the time the Japanese arrived at Midway, they were ill-equipped for the battle to come and the U.S. won a decisive victory from which the Japanese never recovered.

Sin feeds on our emotional vulnerabilities. This doesn't mean that we are to become uncaring robots that are completely free from emotion. What it does mean is that we need to be cognizant of our emotions when we are dealing with stressful situations. We need to learn to take a step back for a moment and collect our thoughts before we make a decision. Rash decisions rarely turn out well. This concept is true for more than just matters of national security. Anytime you're faced with a decision that will have long lasting consequences for you and your family, you need to be in the right state of mind to make the proper decision.

The other issue of national defense and security that needs to be addressed is preparedness. When I wrote *Null and Void,* I had a significant internal debate about the placement of this concept in the book. While I originally covered this in chapter four under the idea of "...*promote the General Welfare...*", I think in hindsight that the topic is better suited to a discussion in terms of defense and security. The fact is that there will always be issues that arise which threaten the physical, emotional and financial security of the United States. This is simply the nature of the sinful world we live in. We live in a world full of violence, disease, and chaos. Failing to properly prepare our government and citizens for these realities is unacceptable.

As I finalize this book, we are beginning to see the early phases of a new virus coming out of China. The states of Washington and New York are already being hit with cases and it will undoubtedly spread to the rest of our nation. As I look back at *Null and Void,* I see my discussion of preparedness and realize how correct I was. I discussed the concept of providing U.S. citizens with debit cards that would provide money that could be used in the event of a national emergency. I wrote about the government stock piling emergency food supplies for citizens in case of shortages and other disasters. Unfortunately, I can see a scenario playing out where the types of programs I proposed could be needed in the near future. We know from our own history that these kinds of events will happen again and failure to prepare for the inevitable is an exercise in foolishness.

The lack of preparation is also an element of sin. We become consumed by our own sinful desires and forget about preparing for the bad times. Studies show that most U.S. citizens do not have enough money in savings to pay a major expense if it were to materialize. Most citizens would be dependent on social safety net programs in the event that they lost their job. Sin provides us with a sense of invincibility in some ways. Our sinful pride makes us believe that the bad things only happen to other people and we will always be okay. However, deep down we all know this isn't true. Unfortunately, even when we do come to
terms with the frailty of our human condition, we are faced with sin exploiting our sense of fear.

The concept of preparing for the trials of life is a double-edged sword when sin is involved. The only way we can hope to overcome these emotions is to have strong relationship with God through Jesus Christ. I will discuss this idea more in a later chapter; however, we need to understand that in order to have the sense of security and peace that we desire, we must have a strong spiritual relationship to serve as our foundation. I'm reminded of the word of Christ in Matthew 7:24-27:

> Therefore whosoever heareth these sayings of mine, and doeth them, I will liken him unto a wise man, which built his house upon a rock: And the rain descended, and the floods came, and the winds blew, and beat upon that house; and it fell not: for it was founded upon a rock. And every one that heareth these sayings of mine, and doeth them not, shall be likened unto a foolish man, which built his house upon the sand: And the rain descended, and the floods came, and the winds blew, and beat upon that house; and it fell: and great was the fall of it.

In this passage Christ is describing the person who fails to build a strong relationship with God during the good times and instead focuses on enjoying life at its best. Our government is created by sinful people in a sinful world and is doomed to fail eventually. When that failure happens, where will you turn?

As we can clearly see, our national security has been eroded by the effects of sin for many years. This is self-inflicted damage caused by an unwillingness to accept that our nation is not perfect. Unfortunately, there are no easy solutions to this problem. Sin will be a factor in how our government functions until Christ returns. Our only hope is to learn to trust in God and focus on developing strategies that mitigate the effects of sin in our decision-making process as much as possible. We will never completely eliminate sin from our government, but by mitigating it as much as possible we can limit the negative impact it has.

Chapter 11:
"… *promote the general welfare…*" Revisited

I received more comments, both positive and negative, regarding this chapter in *Null and Void* than any other. I think the simple reason was because of its discussion of health care reform and my predictions regarding the eventual failure of the Affordable Care Act. At the beginning of that chapter I wrote that the people and the government are inseparable in the United States and the future of our nation would be dependent on the government coming to terms with providing for the best interests of the citizens. Sadly, the U.S. government has not only continued to fail on this account, but has made matters much worse. I've jokingly suggested to some people that I think the Democratic Party read that chapter and had a collective "hold my beer" moment. Virtually every suggest I proposed for fixing the problems in our nation the Democrats attempted to do the exact opposite and made matters worse.

The reason the issue of welfare is so

uncomfortable for many to deal with is because of sin. There are two components to sin's impact on how we deal with issues of human welfare. The first component is greed. For many people, they place their own desires above those of other people. There are so many people who would rather spend an extra $100 a month on a car payment for a luxury car over donating that $100 to a charity to help those in need. What those people don't understand is that they end up paying to help those in need one way or another. Poverty will lead to a whole host of problems that society will inevitably be forced to deal with. The difference is that the longer you put off dealing with the issue, the more money it will cost. On top of that, if the problem gets bad enough the government will be the one dealing with it and the problem will not be solved properly or in a cost-efficient manner. We are much better off allowing non-profits to deal with issues involving welfare than our slow-moving government.

Unfortunately, where we're still seeing this issue most prevalently is within our health care system. The cost of health care continues to go higher and higher with no end in sight. We are to the point that a five-minute CT scan would cost a person without insurance more than a new car. We really need to take a moment to contemplate that reality. That test is essential to a person who is in medical need. Doctors are not ordering CT scans and exposing patients to high doses of radiation on a whim. The doctor is ordering this test because of a medical necessity. On the other hand, you have the option of buying a used car that cost substantially less than a new one. That type of cost saving option is not available for medical care.

In *Null and Void* I quoted Thomas Paine as saying "[t]hat some desperate wretches should be willing to steal and enslave men by violence and murder for gain, is rather lamentable than strange." I used this quote to highlight the fact that our modern medical system has become the new plantation, and I firmly stand by this concept. As a society was cannot thrive as long as people are forced to live in fear for their health. The idea that a single event that is out of their control can bring economic devastation to their family in the blink of an eye is not a viable way of living. More than that it opens the door for sin to take control of a person's life.

I would be more accepting of the medical system we have if it was only having an impact on the choices an individual makes. When I was writing *Null and Void,* I used an example of a 30-

year-old who developed a heart condition. Little did I know at the time that I would end up in a very similar situation when I turned 40. While running a CT scan for another issue, it was discovered that I had a heart anomaly that placed me at increased risk for an aneurysm on my aortic arch. While I was lucky in that it has not developed in to an aneurysm yet, I will require constant monitoring of the condition for the rest of my life. The problem is that I don't have the money for the monitoring and the insurance companies won't cover it.

I'm sure there are many liberals who are laughing at the idea of a conservative being stuck in this situation. However, I still contend now as I did in eight years ago that health care reform is not a partisan issue. For all the good that liberals claimed the Affordable Care Act would do for people, it has made my situation much worse. Previously I may have been able to scrape together the money needed to pay for the tests each year. Now the cost of the tests has become so high that I can't even begin to afford them. All that the Affordable Care Act really did was give the insurance companies and hospitals an excuse to raise the prices on everything. To make matters worse, even if we are able to repeal and replace this legislation, the damage will be done. The price of these

services is not going to come down again. In
fact, any reforms we make at this point will serve
no other purpose than to drive the prices higher.

   This is one of the places where the sinful
concept of greed does so much damage to our
society. The situation I'm in is not about a
choice I made, but because of the sinful
decisions of others I'm left to make a choice no
one should ever have to make. Part of the
reason I'm willing to put myself out here this way
is so that you the reader can come to terms with
how destructive and self-sabotaging sin really is.
The medical community is allowing sin to cloud
their judgment and, in their greed, they are
willing to shorten my life. If the sinful concept of
greed were not consuming their thoughts, they
may realize that keeping me healthy longer, and
paying more taxes would benefit society in the
long run. And while I only represent one case,
there are others in much worse situations than I
am. There are people in this nation who are
being paid not to work by the government due to
medical disabilities. According to the Social
Security Administration there are 8.5 million
people receiving social security disability
insurance payments each year. How many of
those citizens would be capable of holding down
a job if they were able to afford the medical care
they need.

Now I know there are liberals who will claim that the answer to this issue is a socialized medical system where everyone is guaranteed care. However, that system is a liberal pipe dream that has been proven to be unrealistic at best and an absolute disaster at worst. The only way to make socialized medicine work is to limit the care people get. This kind of system creates a eugenics program that is more about meeting liberal desires for population control than it is about providing quality health care for the citizens. If anyone doubts the fact that liberals believe in these kinds of eugenics programs, I would challenge them to look at the history of the Democratic Party in the 1920s and 30s. In fact, many of the ideas the Nazis developed about eugenics came from progressive liberals here in the United States. The Democrat Party's view on eugenics is also what led to abortions becoming some common in the United States.

The bigger problem is that a socialized medical system would require a massive amount of money from taxpayers. The government cannot tax people into morality. This is true of health care, of sin taxes and any other tax designed to address a social condition. The problem with these types of taxes is that they never go to the programs for which they are earmarked and once the government starts using that money for

other programs, they inevitable need to raise taxes more to make up
the difference. If it weren't for taxes on tobacco and alcohol, we wouldn't be able to fund our public schools. To make matters worse, the amount of tax needed would constantly increase as more and more people used the system and would eb compounded by the influx of illegal immigrants who would utilize the system.

We need look no further than to states that have legalized recreational marijuana to see the failure of this type of tax strategy. The citizens of Colorado were told that by legalizing marijuana that the state would be able to tap into a vast taxation resource by taxing the sale of marijuana. What they have found out is quite the opposite. The crime rate has gone up considerably in the years since legalization and has resulted in an increased burden on the criminal justice system. The homelessness problem in Colorado has also increased, which as placed a heavy burden on social services that were already underfunded and stretched thin. This has resulted in Colorado having the highest average local sales tax rate in the nation at 4.73%. Instead of taping into a vast tax resource, the citizens of Colorado are being forced to pay higher taxes to offset the increased costs associated with legalized recreational marijuana use.

While offering universal health care might seem like a good idea to some, the added costs would quickly add up and overburden an already stressed system. The only response the government would have would be to increase taxes. The more you put your trust in the government to take care of you, the more tax dollars the government will require to do so. At some point the law of diminishing returns takes hold. If someone is being taxed at such a high rate that the majority of their pay check goes to the government, then why work at all? If a person can get their needs met without having to exert any effort, then what is the motivation for working? If we were to follow this all the way down the socialist rabbit hole, and tax the rich in a super high tax bracket, then what incentive do we have for them not to move to another country and take their jobs with them. Colorado has also seen this happen as companies moved to states such as Texas for more favorable tax incentives.

All of this is tied back to sin. While there is definitely a need for social safety net programs, they should never be designed as a lifelong solution to societal problems. We have a society where the Democratic Party has used these safety net programs as a form of political capital. When we look at the urban core areas and other locations represented by democrats, we see areas that have high unemployment rates yet the people representing these areas seem to be doing little to bring new jobs to the areas to reduce the dependence on the government. The best example of this was in the fall of 2019 when New York Congresswoman Alexandra Ocasio Cortez fought tax breaks for Amazon to open a distribution center near her district. Congresswoman Cortez did everything she could think of to prevent this center from opening and sadly succeeded. In doing so she ensured that many of her constituents would continue to be beholden to her in some form of twisted political patronage. This seems completely in keeping with a member of the socialist miscreants referred to as "the squad" or as I prefer to call them "the gang of hate".

Another place where we see the impact of sin on our society is in the way some businesses conduct themselves. I've written previously about the concept I refer to as exploitative socialism, and I think this is a good place to reexplore this concept. For those not familiar with this concept, exploitative socialism occurs when a company exploits tax breaks and other development incentives, often times offered by a local or state governments, with the purpose of increasing their profit margin while passing the cost of doing business on to the taxpayers. The example I always use for this is a major national retailer who pays their employees sub minimum wage salaries. This retailer gets away with paying lower wages because their employees earn a commission for every customer who signs up for the company's credit card. Here's where the problem arises. First, the company didn't pay for the building they have, that was covered by the government under STAR bonds, tax increment financing and tax abatements. In other words, the taxpayers paid for the building by offsetting the cost of the building. Second, the company only hires part time employees who are not eligible for benefits. Between the low pay and lack of benefits this results in the taxpayers covering the cost for the employee's health care, food stamps, section 8 housing, and public transportation just to name a few. In this case the company in question has exploited the development incentives and the social safety net programs to get the citizens to pay for the means by which the company is making money, and yet due to the tax abatements, the citizens see next to no return on their investment.

That is a key concept here, that the government is using our tax dollars to invest in these businesses, but is doing little to guarantee a proper return on investment. Programs like tax increment financing, capital improvement districts and STAR bonds are great tools for communities to use to bring new life to areas that are struggling economically. However, when placed in the hands of sinful people who only desire to use those tools for greed, the tool becomes a weapon of oppression and slavery. Many cities have issued these kinds of incentives to developers only to watch in horror as the developers default on whatever payments were meant to be rendered and leave the city's taxpayers holding the bag. This is how we end up with businesses that are deemed "too big to fail", because so much of our tax dollars are tied up in those businesses that if they fail the taxpayers fail also. To make matters worse, in handing out these kinds of incentives we are placing many of our great small business owners in a difficult spot, because they lack the capital necessary to keep up with the larger competition. However, the only reason the competition is larger is because they are fleecing the taxpayers.

If businesses wish for the citizens to help bank roll their projects then they should rightfully expect the citizens to ask for certain conditions to be met. These kind of development incentives should require a business to exceed the minimum wage requirement so that employees are not forced to utilize taxpayer funded subsidies. They need to be providing a full benefits package so the taxpayers are not paying for their employee's health care. They need to be providing tuition reimbursement so that employees have the ability to achieve more in life. All of these changed need to occur because the current situation is not economically sustainable for our nation. We cannot continue to prop up failing businesses and pay for the means of production because someone wants to make more money. Making money is great for our economy, but businesses need to do it on their own instead of looking to the government to do the heavy lifting for them. If a business is unable to survive on its own merits then we need to let it fail so a batter business can come along to replace it. This is how capitalism thrives, is by allowing the weak to fall by the wayside while the innovative succeed.

This brings us to a third issue involving sin, greed and the concept of general welfare. For far too long our nation has been held hostage economically by the Democratic Party and their ridicules notion of how minimum wage should work. The current structure for minimum wage in the United States serves to benefit the progressive socialists in the Democratic Party. The reason for this is that it treats all works the same, like we are part of a socialist collective. This shouldn't be a surprise as the concept of minimum wage that we have today was born out of socialist labor unions that formed in the 1880s and fought for "fair wages" and 40-hour weeks. These groups were drawing there inspiration directly from Karl Marx. Everything about Marx's writing was designed to create a class structure that exemplified the sin nature of humans by creating greed and conflict. If you have any doubts about the power of Marx's words to create this kind of conflict today look at how these concepts are being utilized to argue for a $15/hr. minimum wage for fast food workers.

Unlike the socialist society that Marx envisioned, we are a society of individuals who have distinct needs. The proper answer for our society is a tiered minimum wage system. It doesn't take a genius to figure out that a 17-year-old high school student living at home with their parents does not have the same minimum wage requirement as a 30-year-old widowed mother of three whose husband died fighting to this country. If we created a tiered minimum wage, we would likely be able to reduce the need for SNAP (food stamps) and other societal safety net programs. This is the reason liberal hate this idea so much, because it would result in a lot of people, who are currently accessing services from liberal supported social programs, getting off those programs. The result of this type of program is that the taxpayers would be relieved of some of the financial burden. I would even be open to the idea of offering tax breaks to companies who offer that single mother a job at the increased minimum wage. The reason I can support this tax break is because in addition to the tax dollars the government is saving by not needing to provide those social services to the single mother, the government is also collecting more in payroll and sales taxes due to her increased income. When compared to the amount the government is saving on services and gaining in increased tax revenue, the cost of the tax breaks is minimal. Best of all, since this minimum wage increase is targeted, the rise of inflation is minimized. This concept can be extended further. We could allow businesses that offer tuition reimbursement for college education to pay a lower minimum wage. If a business is going to offer a path for their employees to get ahead, we should reward that business.

One area where we could see a big benefit from this idea would be the establishment of a higher minimum wage tier for college graduates.

The simple truth is that we as a nation have invested a tremendous amount of money at the state and federal level in colleges and universities across this nation. Earlier in this chapter I discussed the concept that the tax money our government spends is an investment into the future of our nation. This being the case, it seems only fitting that we expect a return on that investment. In the case of taxpayer subsidized college education, that means higher incomes and resulting higher payroll taxes. There are a lot of businesses that want the benefits of hiring college graduates, but don't want to pay the wages that come with those benefits. The result is similar to what was discussed earlier about exploitative socialism. In this case the business is exploiting the taxpayers funding of the education system while not paying the wages that will allow the taxpayers to recoup the investment. In public policy this is a phenomenon we refer to as "free riding" and it is generally considered very unethical. We see a similar version of free riding where businesses, and in some cases government entities, only hire highly experienced staff. As a result, someone else has to spend their resources to train staff only to have them hired away by an organization that is unwilling to dedicate the resources necessary to train staff themselves.

When we turn our focus on gaining power and fortune, we allow sin to influence how we interact with others and by extension, how our government interact with us. When the government provides an unfair financial advantage to one business over others and allows that business to develop in ways others cannot, that is no longer capitalism. The concept of capitalism is that if you provide the best service or product available at the best price possible then your business will succeed. If you fail to provide a product or serve the consumer wants at a reasonable price then your business will fail. Under capitalism it is supposed to be the market that determines the success or failure of a business, not the financial interventions of the government. As an economic system, capitalism is designed to be a fluid system that uses innovation to adapt to changing market needs. This is why capitalism is at its best with limited regulation, because regulations stifle innovation and progress. The primary threat to our economy, and by extension or social welfare, is the sinful behaviors of humans. It seems counterintuitive, but the best way to succeed is to stop following after sin and put others first.

Chapter 12:
"*... secure the Blessings of Liberty...*" Revisited

When I originally wrote this chapter in *Null and Void*, I intended it to be about the need to protect the foundations of our freedoms. It was one of the few places in the body of the book that I drew on Christianity explicitly when I quoted Paul in 1st Corinthians 3:10-13:

> According to the grace of God which is given unto me, as a wise masterbuilder, I have laid the foundation, and another buildeth thereon. But let every man take heed how he buildeth thereupon. For other foundation can no man lay than that is laid, which is Jesus Christ. Now if any man build upon this foundation gold, silver, precious stones, wood, hay, stubble; Every man's work shall be made manifest: for the day shall declare it, because it shall be revealed by fire; and the fire shall try every man's work of what sort it is.

I believe more today than eight years ago that this is a great line of scripture to describe the nature of how we are to develop our nation. While we have made some big mistakes, we have also come a long way given the magnitude of sinful obstacles we were forced to overcome.

Unfortunately, we have a growing number of citizens who no longer see this as progress, but want to use the term "progress" for their own twisted purposes. I think the event where this has been seen most clearly in recent events is with the protests at sporting events regarding kneeling for the national anthem. I understand that this is a very delicate subject, so I will be treading very carefully here. Every U.S. citizen has the right to protest their grievances with the government as they see fit as long as it does not infringe on the rights of others. As with all the rights we have as U.S. citizens, the right to protest comes with certain responsibilities. In the case of the First Amendment right to freedom of speech and peaceable assembly, we have the responsibility to recognize that not everyone is going to agree with our position or opinion. We do not have the right to use coercion, violence, intimidation, or fear, in real life or in social media, to force others to accept our position or opinion. Once someone crosses that line, they effectively surrender their position as undefendable, because a position that is defendable does not require such tactics.

When I saw protestors kneeling during the national anthem my memory was drawn back to a man named William Carney. Mr. Carney was a sergeant in the Union Army during the Civil War. In the summer of 1863 Sgt. Carney's unit was involved in a battle against the Confederate Army. At the outset of the battle, the flag bearer for Sgt. Carney's unit was killed. Without hesitation Sgt. Carney dropped his own weapon and took up the unit's U.S. flag and carried it throughout the remainder of the battle, despite being shot three times. When the battle had ended the Confederate Army had managed to hold their ground and Sgt. Carney was forced to retreat by crawling through sand and salt water marshland over one mile to the Union encampment. Despite the pain he endured from his wounds, Sgt. Carney never allowed the U.S. flag to touch the ground, choosing to suffer himself than to allow the flag to be disgraced. For his actions that day, Sgt. William Carney of the 54th Massachusetts Colored Volunteers became the first African-American awarded the Congressional Medal of Honor.

Now we have to realize that Sgt. Carney took this heroic action for the flag of a country where he didn't have the right to vote. A country where he didn't have the right to own property. It was a country that by law only saw him as 3/5th of a person. Despite all of that, Sgt. Carney understood that the U.S. flag stands for something much more than the policies of the moment. The U.S. flag stands for the hope that tomorrow will be better. That no matter how bad today may be, no matter what injustice our society may ignorantly embrace due to our sinful ways, the future will be better. Have we messed up in the past? You bet we have, in more ways than anyone can count. What made our nation great was the underlying Christian foundation that allowed us to overcome our sinful nature. We eventually moved past sinful ideas such as slavery and began to embrace Godly ideas.

Unfortunately, all of this is changing as our society begins to swing back in the other direction. As we begin to adopt more sinful behaviors, we move further away from the ideas that made this nation great. Despite what some people may think, making our nation great again will take a lot more than money, jobs and other metrics of prosperity. Don't forget Paul's words in 1st Timothy 6:10 "For the love of money is the root of all evil: which while some coveted after, they have erred from the faith, and pierced themselves through with many sorrows." If our goal is to make our nation great through sinful greed, the result will be our own destruction.

This is not to say that we need to develop some socialist system where everyone gets what they need. Socialism is not the answer and it never will be. What we need is a system that puts more emphasis on personal growth in the spirit and less on financial growth. A society built around financial prosperity will always result in greed and sinful behavior. I would encourage all of you to look to the model set forth by the early church. Paul describes the early church as the Body of Christ, working together to meet the needs of all believers. The gifts of the Holy Spirit are designed to work together to help each believer as needed. In 1st Corinthians 12:27-28 Paul provides an accounting of the gifts God provides to aid the church:

> Now ye are the body of Christ, and members in particular. And God hath set some in the church, first apostles, secondarily prophets, thirdly teachers, after that miracles, then gifts of healings, helps, governments, diversities of tongues.

When we look at the modern church this is not the model that we are seeing represented. This is a problem for our government because our nation was loosely founded on Christian principles and the churches have always been part of the model on which the government functions. Therefore, if the churches are failing, it only makes sense that the government and society would begin to fail also. It's the Christian idea of Christ conquering sin at the cross that guided our nation to move past sin. What has made our nation great in the past was our ability to overcome the bad and sinful and cherish what is righteous.

As discussed earlier, we have turned church into a social club as opposed to a venue for worshipping God and learning about our spiritual selves. I often see polls that show decreases in church attendance and hear individuals prognosticate about why this is. I find it no coincidence that church attendance has fallen off with the rise of social media's influence on our society. Social media has taken on the twisted role of an online social club. Now people can use any number of social media sites to interact with others and achieve the same goals they were having met when going to a church on Sunday morning. I purposefully use the term "going" as opposed to "attending" because attendance implies active participation in the purpose of the gathering.

In order to turn our nation around we must

first start with repairing the foundation of our nation, and this includes the church. Let's face it, the "blessings of liberty" come from God, and if we want to continue to
have those, then we need to get right with God. This means we get church back to what it's supposed to be. My spirit cringes every time I see a church that spends over half of a Sunday morning service singing music and putting on elaborate productions. The truth is that singing is not a gift of the spirit and the Bible doesn't mention Jesus going around singing songs to people during his ministry. Despite what some believers might think, the life and death of Jesus Christ was not a Broadway musical.

   Much of this is the result of churches ignoring the words of James 2:2-4:

> For if there come unto your assembly a man with a gold ring, in goodly apparel, and there come in also a poor man in vile raiment; And ye have respect to him that weareth the gay clothing, and say unto him, Sit thou here in a good place; and say to the poor, Stand thou there, or sit here under my footstool: Are ye not then partial in yourselves, and are become judges of evil thoughts?

How often it is that churches turn to individuals who have achieved fame and fortune in the sinful world as the leaders of their churches. I've lost count of how many churches I've seen fall into sin by following after the ways of the sinful world. Christ called on his followers to deny ourselves, take up the cross and follow him. A person cannot become wealthy and famous while still denying their own sinful desires, because it is sin that drives them to those seek after fame and wealth. This is why Christ said in Luke 18:25 "For it is easier for a camel to go through a needle's eye, than for a rich man to enter into the kingdom of God." Christ clearly demonstrated that the glorification of God requires personal sacrifice. God is glorified by us coming closer to Him, not by us singing songs or putting on lavish productions. God is not impressed with the trappings of this sinful world.

One of the other problems facing the church today is that many followers of Christ have confused "Christian liberty" with personal liberty. Throughout his epistles Paul says much about the concept of liberty and how it impacts the believer. The fact is that as followers of Christ we are to be of a different mindset than non-believers. We are meant to see the world around us differently from other people. This can be used for good when it allows us to impart godly wisdom to non-believers and help them to come to terms with their own sin. The world does not always see this as good, but it is. When we see someone enslaved by sin, it is part of our nature as Christians to want to free that person from bondage. Unfortunately, the world we live in today often times calls this being "judgmental" or "intolerant". While using those terms might make some liberals feel better about themselves, it doesn't change the fact that God will judge those who have not accepted Christ and, in his judgement, God is very intolerant of sin. From God's perfect point of view the issue of sin is very clear cut and if someone is unwilling to accept their responsibility for their sins then God will not accept them into his kingdom.

Problems arise when we allow our liberties to carry us into things we shouldn't be doing. As Christians we shouldn't be acting as if we are free to do anything we want because Christ has paid the cost for our sins. Christ's sacrifice at the cross does not serve as a blank check for us to do as we wish without facing any consequences. As Paul said in Romans 6:1-2, "What shall we say then? Shall we continue in sin, that grace may abound? God forbid. How shall we, that are dead to sin, live any longer therein?" When we look to continue in sin after accepting Christ, we are in essence saying that we want to nail Christ to the cross over and over again. God understands that we live in a sinful world and as a result we will commit sin from time to time. However, that is a far different situation from the person who treats the sacrifice Christ made with such irreverence as to continue to sin without regard.

The other problem with abusing our liberties is that it opens believers up to hypocrisy. For example, you can't be living in sin and telling others to stop sinning. Christ addressed this issue in Luke 6:39 when he said "Can the blind lead the blind? shall they not both fall into the ditch?" How can anyone hope to lead others to Christ if they are following after sinful ideas? This doesn't just go for the way we interact with strangers, but also how we interact with our own families. If you're a parent and you want your children to come up believing in Christ, then don't engaging in conduct that makes them question the strength of your faith. This is where abusing our Christian liberties and treating them like personal liberties causes trouble because in doing so, we don't just undermine our relationship with God, but the relationships we're in with others as well.

We also must remember that we cannot confuse liberties with perceptions. The fact of the matter is that everyone's perception of the world around them is filtered through the lens of sin. Let's say that you're sitting in a restaurant having dinner and you have a glass of water in front of you. In that same restaurant is a person who has a problem with alcohol and they're really wanting to order an alcoholic beverage. After looking around the restaurant this person sees others drinking what they believe to be alcoholic beverages so they order one also. Now, your argument could be that you were drinking water so you didn't negatively influence that person…but is that true? That person had no idea what was in your glass; it could have been vodka, gin, water, or soda pop. The decision to order that drink was the result of sin's influence on the person's behavior and perception.

Oh, I hear you out there, you're claiming that you wouldn't go to a place that serves alcohol so that could never happen. That's fine, we can run down that rabbit hole. Say you took your family to a local fast food establishment. You're sitting there getting ready to eat when a morbidly obese person walks in. There you are saying grace with your family, sporting your WWJD bracelet and wearing the t-shirt from last summer's church picnic. What is the perception of the obese person? From their perspective God must not have any issues with eating unhealthy food…but is that true? Looking to 1st Corinthians 6:19-20 Paul said:

> What? know ye not that your body is the temple of the Holy Ghost which is in you, which ye have of God, and ye are not your own? For ye are bought with a price: therefore glorify God in your body, and in your spirit, which are God's.

From a certain perspective eating at the fast food restaurant might be more damaging than eating at a restaurant that serves alcohol.

The reality is this, God doesn't want us to do anything to damage the bodies He gave us. As I have long said, if I were to get a tattoo it would say "This body on loan from God". Think of the way you treat your body and then imagine someone borrowing your car and treating it the same way. How would you feel if you owned a nice car and I borrowed it and put cheap gasoline in the tank, messed up the interior and sprayed caustic chemicals all over the paint? I'm sure most of you would be very upset with me. Now imagine how God feels when you do the same to the body he created. I'm fairly confident that most people who read this last paragraph started feeling uncomfortable upon realizing how God perceived the way we tend to treat his creation.

This concept of perception is not in any way new to Christianity. During the early days of the Church, The Roman authorities persecuted Christians over the belief that we were all cannibals because we ate the flesh and drank the blood of Christ. As believers we know that this is purely symbolic and in no way a representation of cannibalism. Regardless of the truth, the perception continued among Roman authorities for some time. This is yet another example of perception being viewed through the biased lens of the sin nature. If a person is devoid of the positive mitigating influence of the Holy Spirit, then the default perception bias will almost always be towards a perception that encourages sinful behavior. This concept is at the very core of the sin nature. Sin thrives on twisting perceptions of the truth. As discussed earlier in this book, God is the source of all truth. Therefore, since sin is the anthesis of God, sin is the corruptor of all truth. We cannot live in truth and ensure liberty when we are allowing sin to twist our perspective of what is true.

The core concepts held within the Christian belief system are essential to the continuation of liberty in our nation. The reason for this is that the concept of liberty is directly tied to freedom of thought. A person who is locked in the

bondage of sin and unable to freely exercise their own thoughts will always be
subject to the twisted perceptions that sin imposes on their mind. No matter how much liberty someone claims to have, if they lack the ability to actually exercise it their liberty is unrealized and non-existent. If our nation is truly dedicated to preserving liberty for future generations, then we need to make confronting sin in our government a common goal that we face with determination and resolve.

So, it seems that we're stuck in a nasty dichotomy with no way out? Not so fast. God did provide Judges to the Israelites before they demanded a king and we can follow a similar model. The goal of our nation should be to elect godly men and woman to office who understand the nature of the sinful illness we are faced with. We've had a group of Conservative Christians in the United States who have been pushing for these types of elected officials for years. In order for our government to work properly we need Christians who understand the problem in place to help create the solution.

This concept goes against everything that liberalism stands for. I can already hear the far-left crying foul over the idea of people running our government using faith-based principles. The very first complaint that will come from the left will be the need for separation between church and state. The problem is that this separation has been perverted by the left to stand for something our nation's founders never intended. We are not talking about the

government violating the establishment clause of the First Amendment. Nowhere in The U.S. Constitution is there any stipulation that elected officials are not allowed to be public servants and servants of God at the same time. Despite what the far left wants us to believe, there is no prohibition against elected officials, or any other government employee for
that matter, engaging in religious practices.

To understand this matter we need to take a critical look at the First Amendment and understand exactly what our founding fathers wrote about government and religion. This means looking at the true meaning behind the First Amendment's application to religion and understanding the context in which the amendment was created.

In the decades leading up to the Revolutionary War the predominant church in the colonies was the Church of England, with the monarch, King George III as the head of the church. By decree of the British government, all people living in the colonies were required to pay a tax to help fund the state sponsored church. The idea of being forced to provide financial support to the Church of England was found to be very offensive to the many colonists who had fled religious persecution in Great Britain. It should go without saying that if you are fleeing a church that has persecuted you, the last thing you want is to be forced to pay taxes to support that church. Imagine the outrage if the Catholic Church was allowed by law to require everyone, including the victims of pedophile priests, to money for the up keep on their churches. One of our nation's founding fathers, Patrick Henry, actually, fought a court battle over this very issue in the Virginia colony. While Henry lost the case, the presiding judge only awarded the Church of England one penny in symbolic compensation.

To make matters worse, religious institutions in the colonies outside of the Church of England were required by the Stamp Act to pay taxes for many paper products. Imagine your church being required to pay a separate tax for each Bible, hymnal, book or Sunday church bulletin that it uses. Today such a tax would be especially burdensome to faith-based groups who provide free or low-cost Bibles to various groups in our communities. Thankfully the framers of the Constitution saw the need to correct such a problem.

The way the freedom of religion element in the First Amendment is written has made it complicated to say the least. There are a number of different elements that factor into the freedom of religion as it applies under the First Amendment, but two of the most cited are the "Establishment Clause" and the concept known as "The Wall of Separation." The legal standing for the Establishment Clause has traditionally been viewed as very clear. James Madison, in crafting the First Amendment, wrote "[c]ongress shall make no law respecting an establishment of religion, or prohibiting the free exercise thereof…". The commonly held belief is that this line prohibits the U.S. government from establishing a religion. This particular view of the "Establishment Clause" is the result of a 1947 decision by the United States Supreme Court in the case of *Everson v. Board of Education*.

I contend that the interpretation of the First Amendment that the high court relied on for the *Everson v. Board of Education* decision was flawed. Progressive liberals, who comprised the majority of the justices on the U.S. Supreme Court in 1947, have taken the word "establishment" in this context to mean creation. However, in reading Madison's words, it's clear that he actually intended the word "establishment" to mean either a structure, business or other institution, similar to a bar being called a "drinking establishment".

This reading of the First Amendment is further confirmed when we look at the punctuation Madison used. Let's look at the First Amendment in its entirety:

> Congress shall make no law respecting an establishment of religion, or prohibiting the free exercise thereof; or abridging the freedom of speech, or of the press; or the right of the people peaceably to assemble, and to petition the Government for a redress of grievances.

 Between the words "…establishment of religion…" and "…or prohibiting…" Madison has placed a comma, denoting that the words following the comma were part of the same concept. Compare this with the words "…exercise thereof…" and "…or abridging…" which are separated by a semicolon, denoting two distinctly different ideas. In order to accept the liberal misinterpretation of the First Amendment we would be forced to accept that Madison viewed the supposed prohibition of a state sponsored religion and the protection of religious expression as being connected concepts, which they clearly are not.

Furthermore, in order to interpret the line "[c]ongress shall make no law respecting an establishment of religion…" the way liberals have, we would need to view the word "establishment" as a verb, which is inconsistent with the placement of the indefinite article "an" before the word "establishment".   In order for the liberal interpretation to be true, the word "establishment" would need to be preceded by the adverb "the".

If any further evidence was needed to illustrate that the First Amendment has been misinterpreted by the left, we need look no further than Madison's other writings in the U.S. Constitution. Nowhere in his writings does Madison connect a prohibitive clause and a protective clause in the same concept. Madison is very careful to keep prohibited and protective clauses separate to prevent confusion. The proper reading of the freedom of religion section of the First Amendment should be: Congress shall create no law that interferes with religious institutions, beliefs, or the free expression of faith through associated activities. I have no doubt that this reading is completely in keeping with what Madison intended.

Unfortunately, the far left, either by malicious intent or illiteracy, have completely twisted the meaning of the First Amendment and infringed on millions of citizens religious liberties. To compound the problem, the misinterpretation of the First Amendment influenced the reading of

Thomas Jefferson's letter to the Danbury Baptist which gives us the idea of a "…wall of separation between Church & State." Given the proper reading of the First Amendment we can now reframe the context in which we view the "wall of separation".

The design of the First Amendment is such as to guarantee citizens the right to freely express their religious beliefs. Furthermore, the First Amendment does not guarantee a protection of "freedom from religion" whereby a person is protected from ever being exposed to religious ideas and beliefs. The very notion of that is ludicrous and goes against everything the First Amendment stands for.   The First Amendment also does not curtail religious expression based on the status of a person's employment with the government. By extension it means that with a proper interpretation of the First Amendment, the government cannot compel a government employee to violate their religious beliefs.

Issues of religious liberties will continue to be a problem in our nation. The far left is obsessed with placing restrictions on religion, particularly Christianity. We have reached a point in the United States where the government is being challenged regarding religious imagery on memorials to the dead. State universities are being challenged for having volunteer, non-denominational chaplains for sports teams. For the far left this isn't a matter of trying to contain religious belief, but a veiled attempt at eliminating religious belief. The First Amendment is all that stands in the way of liberals banishing faith from the public square.

Section Three:
The Liberal Problem

Chapter 14:
Liberals and Sin, Why Don't They Understand?

Believe it or not, liberals do believe in sin…they just don't realize it. The way people react to sin can take on many different forms. A lot of these differences are the result of how sin acts in each person's life. Just as sin impacts each person differently, the reaction people have towards sin can be vary widely also. For liberals, they react by seeking to correct the issue of sin by turning back time. Liberals want us to believe that in their sinful state that they will create a perfect socialist utopia. What they don't understand is that it took a perfect, sinless God to create the previous utopia, the Garden of Eden. The liberal belief goes something like this: if humans can recreate the perfect utopia God created in the garden and live a life free of sin, then God will forgive the sins and all will be right again.

The problem with this belief is multifold. First, the sin nature found in humans will never allow the envisioned liberal utopia to come into existence. Sin is going to drive people to do things that are against their own good. No child grows up wanting to be a drug addict and no one thinks that becoming addicted to a substance is a good idea. People end up dealing with addictions because they are looking for an answer to some aspect of the sin that is infecting their life. The one part of sin that is completely incompatible with the liberal ideology is that sin is not equal. God's version of equality looks very different from what liberals want to see. From God's perspective the more you are entrusted with the more God expects of you. As a result, God expects more from some people and provides more blessings to some people. Progressive liberals want everyone to be treated equally regardless of reality.

Some people need more blessings to fulfill God's plan for their life. While God allows us free will, God also has certain ideas that he wants us to accomplish once we accept Christ. This concept is completely foreign to many liberals. From the perspective of liberal ideology, God should be allowing us to make all of our own decisions and treat us the same regardless of how bad those decisions are. Have you ever noticed that the Christians who are most hated by liberals are the really successful Christians? This is not by happenstance, but the result of sin guiding people to hate that which proves that sin is wrong.

The second problem with the liberal belief of creating a utopia is that it revolves around a lie. If the truth sets us free, then the lies of sin imprison us! The utopia that liberals seek to create is based on their own vision and their misguided belief that everyone wants the same thing they do. We saw something similar playout during the run up to the impeachment hearings against President Trump. Liberals were convinced that there was evidence to remove President Trump from office, even before he was sworn in. President Trump never had a chance to govern before the Democratic Party was trying to create a false narrative to argue for his removal from office. The more we learn about the false impeachment we are starting to realize that individuals within foreign governments were funneling money to the Democratic Party for the purpose of destabilizing the United States. The far left of the Democratic Party could care less about what others believe; they are only concerned with their own desires. To this extent liberals seek opportunities to control others in order to achieve their goal of creating a utopia.

In essence, liberals believe that they are God!

Yet in their arrogance, hubris and pride they continue to strive towards a goal they will never attain by themselves. Sadly, deep down inside this element of the liberal belief exists the liberal's desire to be closer to God. This desire to be closer to God but refusal to accept God's control lies at the very core of the sin nature. I've lost track of the number of times if watched as people try to run away from God. Even in their most dire of circumstances, people would rather maintain the illusion of being in control than admit that God is truly in charge.

The best word to describe how liberals feel towards sin is desperate. Since liberals believe in sin on some level and know it's destructive consequences, they also know the need to deal with those consequences before it's too late. Unfortunately, since all of their schemes to counteract the consequences of sin fail, they become more desperate as time goes on. Each failure brings them closer to one of two outcomes: 1) the forced realization that Christ is the only answer, or 2) the return of Christ, in which case it will be too late. Deep in their psyche liberals know that their time to deal with the issue of sin is running out.

The third problem liberals have with the concept of sin is that it's dependent on a perfect world. From the stand point of modern liberalism, the world should be a perfect place where everyone acts according to set social norms. Unfortunately, we do not live in a perfect world and social norms vary from one segment of society to another.

This constant change in social norms makes people uncomfortable, especially liberals. For liberals everything has to fit into a neat little box. When we look at the groups the comprise the liberal agenda, we see this constant need to identify with something. No one is allowed to simply be "human". To make matters worse, liberals are constantly adding new identities to categorize people into. This has evolved into people identifying as a horse, cow, dog, deer or unicorn. This is all very convenient in that it allows someone to distance themselves from the concept of sin. After all, animals are not in sin, so there was no need for Christ to die for them. Therefore, if someone identifies as an animal, in their mind they have no need for salvation.

The liberal desire to categorize everyone has results in their propensity to label everything that does not conform to their ideology as "hate". The irony of this is profound as the beliefs liberals often find themselves protecting and endorsing are often associated with sin, which includes hate. This reminds me of the events of Matthew 12:25-26:

> And Jesus knew their thoughts, and said unto them, Every kingdom divided against itself is brought to desolation; and every city or house divided against itself shall not stand: And if Satan cast out Satan, he is divided against himself; how shall then his kingdom stand?

If the ultimate source for the argument's liberals make is found in the context of sin, how can those arguments be anything but hateful? Sin hates humanity, so does it not make sense that an argument found in the context of sin is in essence designed to destroy humanity? As I mentioned in chapter 5, why would anyone not want Christ to be real? Why wouldn't someone want their sins forgiven? Furthermore, why wouldn't someone want to extend that to the rest of humanity?

Liberals cannot tolerate the idea that God sent his only son to die for our sins. The reason for this is that if God did send his son to die for our sins, that would mean that all the plans liberals have for recreating a perfect utopia free from sin are bound to fail. Liberals don't like the idea of being required to follow God's rules. Liberals want to determine what is and is not sinful. The problem with this concept is rather obvious…it's their own sin nature pushing them towards this idea. Sin will always convince people to do things they shouldn't be doing. Given enough time to work, sin will convince people to kill each other and kill themselves. This is why we see the most hardened liberals promoting sinful ideas like abortion. Only sin could convince people to believe that killing your own people off is a good idea. Liberals believe that the more people there are, the harder it is for them to control those people. This is the same mentality that the democrat slave owner had on his plantation. The democrats see population as a balancing act. They need enough of us to complete the work they are unwilling to do themselves, but they also need to limit the numbers so that we don't become mindful of what they are doing and revolt against their system.

The sinful nature of humans will always drive us to falsely believe that we are capable of determining what is sinful. This belief is like allowing an alcoholic to set the blood alcohol level that will be used to determine if someone is driving under the influence. If the standard is being set by sinful humans, then the standard is always going to be set so low that nothing would be sinful. This is a prime example of why God never intended humans to govern ourselves.

We simply lack the fortitude necessary to hold ourselves responsible. We see this all the time with corrupt politicians and government employees. To make matters worse, as we began to lose faith in our government years ago, we turned to the news media to hold the government accountable. However, as we've seen all too often in recent years, the news media has fallen victim to the same corrupt influence of sin.

Not all people see sin as a problem. For some people the concept of sin having a controlling influence over their life, even if unrealized, is comforting. This is what you have with many atheists and agnostics. Sin is still a very powerful influence in their lives, but they choose to ignore it. Imagine this spiritual life as a mundane, repetitive job. When sin is in control you don't have to think as much because sin does the thinking for you. This is the kind of collective "group think" that promotes and drives the liberal ideology. When people abandon their own thoughts to the thoughts of others, they become more susceptible to the influence of sin in their lives. The task of preventing sin from encroaching into our lives is a daily struggle. For many people they would prefer to avoid this struggle and allow others to make those decisions for them. This is another aspect of sin, where people become lazy and don't want to put in the work to fight the effects of sin in their life.

In thinking about the people who refuse to challenge sin in their lives, we can look to the words of Christ as an example of this. The first example we have is from the Parable of the Minas in Luke 19. In this parable three servants are given money before their lord travels to a far land. Upon returning the first two servants present their lord with the money he had given them to invest and the money the they had earned through those investments. As a result, their lord provided these two men with rewards equivalent to the good work they had done. However, when the third servant can we see the following occur in Luke 19:20-26:

> And another came, saying, Lord, behold, here is thy pound, which I have kept laid up in a napkin: For I feared thee, because thou art an austere man: thou takest up that thou layedst not down, and reapest that thou didst not sow And he saith unto him, Out of thine own mouth will I judge thee, thou wicked servant. Thou knewest that I was an austere man, taking up that I laid not down, and reaping that I did not sow: Wherefore then gavest not thou my money into the bank, that at my coming I might have required mine own with

> usury? And he said unto them that stood
> by, Take from him the pound, and give it
> to him that hath ten pounds. (And they
> said unto him, Lord, he hath ten pounds.)
> For I say unto you, That unto every one
> which hath shall be given; and from him
> that hath not, even that he hath shall be
> taken away from him.

What we see here is a servant, who like many liberal voters, is lazy and unwilling to put in the work. The end result for these voters is the same as it is for the servant, they are left with nothing. Liberals purposefully look to keep people indebted to their ideological system. This leaves people unable to pull themselves out of the circumstances created by liberal policies.

This problem was created because we have been putting our faith in in other sinful humans instead of God. Nothing good is going to happen when you place a sinful person on a pedestal. A sinful person, given power and prestige, will almost never be able to maintain the moral high ground without a lot of help from God. Since sin feeds on the power and prestige, the person's perception becomes twisted so that they feel they don't need God. This is the conundrum that is created within liberalism. Everything about the liberal ideology is counter to the truth. Liberals know that sin is present, but refuse to admit that its present. This results in an ideology that focuses on fixing the flaws of humanity while ignoring the true nature of the flaws. When liberals are inevitably unable to fix those flaws their ideology then turns to removing the flaw. The only way to remove the flaw is to dehumanize people and create an intellectual class of elites who view themselves as better than everyone else. The end result is one sin on top of another, and another, and another. Nothing good will ever come from developing a government or society in that way.

As I have already established, God never intended humans to self-govern, so we're on slippery ground to begin with. When we add in a government following a liberal ideology that promotes a belief founded in sin, the end result is not going to be something beneficial to humanity. It will inevitably become a society that sees humanity in the lowest term possible. The goal being to convince us that we are unworthy of God's love and salvation, which is simply not true. This is why it is so essential that we hold to the idea of human worth no matter what lies the far-left tries to force upon us.

Chapter 15: Liberalism and Christ

There are many complex reasons why liberals attack Christianity more than any other religion. However, all of these reasons can be traced back to the same basic idea of wanting people to be enslaved, be that to other people or to sin. Let's not forget that the Democratic Party was the party of slavery, Jim Crow, the KKK, and numerous other hateful institutions that have developed in the course of our nation's history. The more the far-left can effectively marginalize Christianity, the longer they can pursue their hateful agenda. The hope is that eventually they will wear down Christians to the point that we will simply give up. Fortunately for humanity, that is not going to happen.

One of the most perplexing elements of the far lefts attacks on Christianity is not the actual attacks but the fact that they refuse to accept God's free gift of salvation. Let's be honest, who wouldn't want their sins forgiven? The cause and effect are rather simple: accept Christ, be forgiven of your sins, be a person changed for the better in this world and have eternal life in the world to come. It takes a very different person to not see that as being positive for society. And yet, we see a large swath of our society that is not only unwilling to accept Christ, but is actively working to prevent others from accepting Christ also. This is about much more than freedom of choice or God's creation of humanity to have free will the liberal ideology is about actively seeking the destruction of humanity. When we look at the liberal ideology, we the results of accepting sin and allowing sin to take control of a society.

In analyzing the actions of the far-left, we quickly see this common thread of stopping the spread of Christianity. The goal of stopping the spread of Christian beliefs is central to the liberal ethos because the liberal ideology is founded on continuing to keep people enslaved to their own sins. While stopping the spread of Christianity is central to the liberal ideology, there are a number of different vectors by which they approach this goal. The most overt way this occurs is by suppressing Christian activity in the public sphere of influence. This form of suppression takes on many forms, from simple intimidation to frivolous lawsuits and even suppressing the First Amendment rights of Christians on social media platforms.

The most prevalent form of this is organizations attacking government entities for even the loosest association with Christianity. Interestingly enough, Islamic, Jewish and other faiths don't seem to be attacked on these same grounds. For example, state universities are allowed to have rooms for Islamic prayer without repercussions. However, if that same university wants a room for Christian prayer it must be called an "interfaith" area. The goal of this is to water down Christian beliefs with the beliefs of other faiths with the hope of suppressing Christian beliefs.

Additionally, the far left has taken to utilizing the LGBT community to launch their attacks on Christianity. These attacks seek to suppress the Christian community from discussing the concept of sin in general. While it might look as if they are only attacking the idea of calling same sex relations a sin, the reality of this attack is far broader. The goal of the far-left is to slowly erode all sin until there is nothing left for Christ to have died for. This is the deception of sin at work in our world. As I demonstrated in chapter one, all sin is the same in God's eyes, thus when humans seek to erode part of it, we seek to erode all of it. Ultimately the erosion of sin leads to people feeling that they don't need Christ because there is no sin to begin with, thus achieving the goal of sin, to convince us that there is no need for salvation.

One of the more deceptive ways the far left has sought to suppress the spread of Christianity is through the creation of fake "Christian" groups. I've spoken about this is previous books, but this form of suppression is so unique and dangerous that it needs to be discussed again. Liberals often use hate groups and cults disguised as "Christian" organizations to create the false impression that Christianity is a hateful religion. We have seen a number of these groups come to the fore front over the last few decades, many of them offering up very vocal and public accusations against specific segments of society. Most of these groups are supported privately by the far-left and are designed specifically to create public animosity towards the Christian faith.

One of the earliest attempts at this was the People's Temple and its infamous founder Jim Jones. The ties between Jim Jones and the far left are known but not widely reported or documented. Part of the problem with drawing a clear connection between Jones' cult and the Democratic Party is that the Carter Administration classified more than 5,000 pages of documents related to the People's Temple and other issues associated with Jim Jones activities. It's still unclear why these documents were classified by the Carter Administration, but it certainly raises suspicions as to how the Democratic Party was involved in the cult. What we do know for certain is that many active members of the Democratic Party today went on record during the early to mid-1970s in support of Jim Jones. We also know that Jim Jones was not preaching Christianity. While in his early years Jim Jones attempted to align his organization with various mainline protestant churches, his message was decidedly not that of Christianity. In fact, during sermons Jones would claim that the Bible was nothing more than a tool of slavery that had been in use for over 2,000 years. And yet, to this day the left leaning media continues to erroneously portray Jim Jones and the Jonestown commune as a far-right Christian group. This was evident most recently in late 2018 when a cable television network produced a drama about Jonestown and the "t" in the middle of the title "Jonestown" was fashioned in the shape of a Christian cross.

These types of attacks on Christianity will likely become more prevalent in the future. We could easily point to this as the fulfillment of prophecy, and it might well be. This idea goes directly to what I discussed in chapter 7 of my previous book *Governance by Addiction*, that the addict thought process leads liberals to attack any idea that they believe threatens their perception of reality. The problem is that their perception of reality is flawed due to sin. Our sin nature does not want us to accept Christ. Our sin nature wants us to be miserable and living in sin. It's our sin nature that is self-sabotaging us when we try to succeed in life. It's our sin nature that drives us to do things that will hurt the people we love. It's also part of our humanity's sin nature to attack what we know in our conscience is right.

In John 15:18 Christ warned us that these kinds of persecutions would come to pass when he said "If the world hate you, ye know that it hated me before it hated you." The world is a sinful place that hates righteousness, because the world hates anything that is contradictory to sinful ways of the world. Many of us who believe in Christ have been persecuted for our beliefs, even if we didn't realize it. I have no doubt that I've been turned down for jobs and promotions at work, among other things, because of my faith in Christ. However, I take comfort knowing that if God had wanted me to be in those positions, he would have made it happen. I thank God that I may not know what his plan is, but I know that God does have a plan.

This exposes one of the aspects that liberals have a problem with concerning Christianity. As believers we know that God has a plan and are willing to accept God's plan regardless of our own wants and desires. We are willing to put our free will on the backburner and go along with God's will because we know that in his infinite wisdom, God's plans are always much better than anything we can come up with. Liberals on the other hand are empowered by their own sinful beliefs that their plans are far superior to anything God can come up with. More than that, they actually resent God's plans based on the sinful belief that God's plans are detrimental to humanity. This concept makes no sense as God created humanity and wants us to succeed. This would be like a child claiming that their parent wants bad things for them. And while there are some sad situations where parents do thing that are not in their child's best interest, this is always because of the influence of sin in the parent's life. Liberals seem to confuse Satan's desire for us to fail with God's desire for humanity to succeed.

Liberals feel a certain sense of resentment towards God because of the events that transpired in the Garden of Eden. This is once again, an example of the prideful nature of sin. For many liberals they refuse to see humanity as being at fault but would rather blame God for allowing sin to enter the world. Liberals even take this line of thinking a step further and argue that God did not create humanity, but that is was primordial goo that evolved into humans. The problem is that if you go far enough back in time you will reach a moment when the only answer you have is to accept that some outside force acted upon creation. Looking at the Big Bang as an example we see an event where liberals claim the entirety of the universe was created in a giant vacuum in space when a single particle exploded. If this is the case, then where did all the matter within the universe come from? While we might be able to explain the appearance of one particle in a vacuum utilizing Heisenberg's Uncertainty Principle, it hardly accounts for all of the matter in the universe. And if we're going to argue that all of the matter in the universe was confined to that one area of space where the Big Bang occurred, then how would it have been able to escape the force of its own gravity. Afterall, that would amount to the largest black hole ever to exist. In essence what scientists want us to believe is that all of the matter currently in the universe appeared out of nothing, without any gravitational impact on the sounding space or time and upon exploding seeded matter in all of the universe. If this is the case then we should be seeing black holes exploding in the universe on a regular basis as they absorb so much matter as to reach some type of critical mass. We know this is not the case as black holes are suspected of losing matter over time through a phenomenon known as black body radiation. This sounds like a very convenient explanation for when they really don't have answers. It also sounds like the kind of answer sin would create to drive away the truth.

   This is but one example of how the far-left uses partial truths to confuse the public regarding issues. Liberalism thrives on using sin to twist our perspective and makes it difficult for us to determine what is true. I know this sounds like a broken record at this point, but it bears repeating…the liberal ideology exists because of sin. The last thing liberals want is for you to be free from your sins and capable of making choices that are your own. Individuality is a direct threat to liberal desires for power and control over people. Christianity, and all of the truths associated with Christianity, are in direct opposition to the liberal belief that liberals are capable of solving the problem of sin outside of God.

Chapter 16:
The Liberal Attack on Christianity

In chapter two of my book *Governance by Addiction*, I discussed the various ways that liberals utilize lies to twist the perception we have of the truth. The use of lies for this purpose is the direct result of sin for two reasons. First, sin finds itself at home in lies and deceit. God exists in pure truth so the last thing sin wants is to offer up the truth which will push people further towards God. Secondly, our sin nature wants to follow after a lie over the truth. Imagine that you're trying to convince someone to do something and they are from a foreign country and speak another language. Trying to convince them in English would be difficult. However, you would have a much easier time if you are speaking their native language. Similarly, sin offers us lies because we naturally want to believe the lies around us. This is why as Christians we find it so difficult to understand why some liberals believe some of the ideas they do. As a Christian it seems unrealistic to think that humans could ever create a perfect "socialist paradise", and yet many liberals will be in tears over the belief that this fantasy can happen. This is especially powerful when the lie is repeated over and over again. The far-left is very adapted at using this type of repetition as a form of hypnosis to convince the masses to follow after their lies and misleading beliefs. This is where the famous quote from Joseph Stalin comes from, that "a lie told often enough becomes the truth".

I think it's important to look at the way liberals lie about Christianity and why these attacks are so powerful in influencing the masses. We do not naturally seek to have our short comings and flaws pointed out for all to see. The idea of having to come to terms with our own sinful conduct is easily exploited by those who wish to undermine the tenets of Christianity. In this environment it's easy to see how the lies and disinformation of the far left can lead many people to see Christianity as an antiquated set of beliefs that have no influence on the world today.

For example, it's sin that ultimately leads nations to seek conquest, riches and control over other people. It's sin that leads one group of people to believe that they are superior to another. It's sin that results in people believing that they are able to self-govern, even when it's obvious that they can't. I realize this is counter to everything the far left has been preaching to society for years about religion in general and Christianity in particular. The notion the far left wants the world to believe is that religion is antiquated and backwards resulting in it being the antithesis of progress. However, nothing could be further from the truth.

To truly understand the progressive nature of Christianity we must separate God's plan for salvation from the sinful actions of humanity. The perfect example of this is the crusades which took place during the middle ages. Clearly the God who sent his only begotten son to die for the sins of humanity did not tell the leaders of the Catholic Church to invade other regions and slaughter the inhabitants of those regions as liberals would have us believe. While I could cover a long list of transgressions committed by people over the years claiming to be Christians, I'd be treading over some well-worn ground. It is sin that tells people to wage war or destroy others, not God. God's message to humanity is the same today as it was when Christ left this earth. I Matthew 28:18-20 Christ said:

> …All power is given unto me in heaven and in earth. Go ye therefore, and teach all nations, baptizing them in the name of the Father, and of the Son, and of the

Holy Ghost: Teaching them to observe all things whatsoever I have commanded you…"

Nowhere in those instructions does Christ call for his followers to makes war, kill people, or place people in bondage. Within the confines of the new covenant created at the cross, God will not tell us to destroy his creation.

With this in mind I want to look at some of the areas where the far left misleads the public about Christianity. The first idea is that Christianity is misogynistic. The basis of this believe is that many churches do not allow women to hold leadership roles in the church. There are two versus from scripture, both written by the Apostle Paul, which gave rise to this idea. First is 1 Corinthians 14:33-35:

For God is not the author of confusion, but of peace, as in all churches of the saints. Let your women keep silence in the churches: for it is not permitted unto them to speak; but they are commanded to be under obedience as also saith the law. And if they will learn any thing, let them ask their husbands at home: for it is a shame for women to speak in the church.

The second passage is found in 1 Timothy 2:9-12:

> …in like manner also, that the women adorn themselves in modest apparel, with propriety and moderation, not with braided hair or gold or pearls or costly clothing, but, which is proper for women professing godliness, with good works. Let a woman learn in silence with all submission. And I do not permit a woman to teach or to have authority over a man, but to be in silence.

Reading these two sections of scripture alone without the context in which Paul was writing would easily lead us to believe that women are not allowed to speak in the church. The problem is that just about everything else Paul wrote contradicts these two passages of scripture.

In Romans 16:1 Paul recognizes Phoebe as being a woman who has done great works for the early church. In Romans 16:6 Paul makes mention of a woman named Mary also. Paul makes mention of Timothy's grandmother Lois and mother Eunice as being faithful and involved with the church. Paul even makes mention of women praying and prophesizing in 1 Corinthians 11. This makes sense as we're told in Acts 21:8-9 that Paul stayed in Caesarea with Philip the Evangelist who had four daughters who were prophets.

So, knowing that the word of God is infallible, how do we reconcile this clear discrepancy. We accomplish this by looking at the context in which Paul is writing both of these letters. God's plan for Paul is what placed him in the situation that is the basis for the context in which he was writing these letters for a reason. To ignore the context of Paul's writing is in effect to ignore God's will. In both cases Paul is writing in letters to churches suffering trials of faith due to the sinful influences of the world. The early church, much like we do today, struggled with living in a sinful world. Paul was looking to address specific issues he was seeing in the churches. One of these issues can be seen in 1 Timothy 5:13 when Paul wrote of women "…wandering about from house to house, and not only idle but also gossips and busybodies, saying things which they ought not." Here we see Paul providing evidence of a sinful act that was causing problems in these churches. Clearly there was a problem with women gossiping in the church and it was probably causing some degree of tension. I think this idea is reinforced by Paul's mention of the way women were dressing in 1 Timothy 2:10. Based on the context I think Paul is implying that people should be focused on worship when at church and not on gossiping about what clothes someone else wore to the market last week.

Paul's complaint here aligns closely with something I mentioned earlier about the church becoming a place of socialization and networking more than a place to worship God. Church should be much more than a place to be seen on Sunday morning. Church is meant to be your opportunity to strengthen your relationship with God through the Holy Spirit and reinforce your faith before going out into the sinful world. We call the main room of a church a sanctuary for a reason. It is supposed to provide a source of protection and reprieve from all of the sin in the world around us. If your goal in attending church is to better your position in life, gain a position of power or boost your personal brand so you can get elected to political office, then you're going to church for the wrong reasons. Doing yourself a disservice is bad, interfering with God's simply compounds the problem. While you are forcing yourself into positions at the church to achieve your goals, you're preventing others from utilizing their gifts of the Holy Spirit to help build their faith and help the body of Christ grow.

The second area to discuss is the concept of inclusion and acceptance in Christianity. I challenge anyone to read the teachings of Jesus Christ and then find a religion more accepting of people who are in sin. The problem is not

Christianity's ability to accept people, but the inability of some people to accept their own sin. Earlier in this book I discussed the concept of Mary Shelley's book Frankenstein being a metaphor for a life in sin. In chapter three of the book we're told of how a young Dr. Frankenstein came to the university at Ingolstadt, and soon after arriving he is told by Professor M. Krempe that everything he has learned about science is wrong. Professor M. Krempe quickly sets about providing Frankenstein with a list of books to read as part of a program to correct his errant education. However, instead of embracing this new found knowledge, Frankenstein rebels against it because the university was unaccepting and no inclusive of his beliefs, no matter how wrong the beliefs were. Ultimately this leads to Frankenstein creating his monster and his eventual destruction. The life of Dr. Frankenstein serves as an allegory for the life of someone who rejects Christianity. We all go through an age of innocence as children, we all come to know that we are in sin. Unfortunately, some of us refuse to accept Christ, choosing to set out on their own while compounding their sin nature until they ultimately die alone without ever knowing God.

As a religion Christianity is very open and inclusive, but with a caveat, you have to be willing to accept Christianity, which means accepting that you're in sin and repent. We see this in the gospels multiple times as Jesus went out amongst all manner of sinners and never turned anyone away. However, there seems to be a double standard when it comes to inclusion and Christianity. According to the far-left, Christians are supposed to accept everyone, regardless of their decision to continue living in sin. This creates a situation similar to what Paul is writing about in 1 Corinthians, where the church is struggling due to the influence of sin. We cannot maintain the church as a sanctuary from sin if we are welcoming sin into the church with open arms. I'm reminded of Paul's words from 1 Corinthians 15:33 "Do not be deceived: "Evil company corrupts good habits." The point is that if you allow sin to take hold in the church then sin will become the nature of the church. Sin filled churches cause many of the problems that are often cited with Christianity, not the Christian faith itself.

We have to remember that Satan did not create sin, he simply exploited God's creation of free will to cause us to create sin. God provides us with the ability to combat sin in our lives, but just as we created sin, it is our responsibility to accept Christ and fight against sin. To this end, it's not the denomination of the church that is the issue, it's the involvement of the Holy Spirit with the church that determines how effective the church is at combating sin. If a church follows liberal beliefs and is more concerned with worldly endeavours, it will become more accepting of sin, then that church will struggle with sin within the church. On the other hand, if a church is more willing to confront sinful behaviour, then the church will be a lot more firmly rooted in its beliefs.

A church firmly rooted in Christian beliefs is the last thing liberals want. The ability to make individuals decisions that are not under the influence of sin is never going to lead to liberals having power. True faith in the finished work of Christ is the anthesis of everything liberalism stands for. We must come to terms with the knowledge that the liberal attacks on our faith will continue and that we need to put follow the example Paul set forth in Ephesians 6:10-20 and put on the Armor of God each and every day.

Chapter 17:
Sin is Irrelevant

In chapter eight of *Governance by Addiction* I discussed the idea that many liberals feel that the "law is irrelevant" in regards to their political ambitions. In writing that chapter I drew from the infamous incident on May 19th 2013 when White House Spokesman Dan Pfefiffer appeared on ABC News's "This Week with George Stephanopoulos" to discuss the IRS targeting of conservative groups. Mr. Pfefiffer famously stated, "I can't speak to the law. The law is irrelevant…". As shocking as this statement is, it's hardly surprising. Afterall, God's word is the ultimately law and God determines what is and is not sin. Yet liberals routinely ignore God's will in favor of their own will. Unable to overcome the effects of sin, many on the far-left have adopted the theory that simply accepting sin will make sinful actions better. From the liberal perspective, most sin is irrelevant. But more than just being irrelevant, liberals want to redefine what is and is not sin.

Let me be clear about this issue from the start. If some action or idea is listed as sinful in the Bible, then it's a sin. If you tell me it's not, then you better show me the nail holes in your hands where you were crucified for the sins of humanity. By virtue of Christ dying for the sins of humanity, Christ gets to determine what is and is not a sin. I can think of nothing more sinful than to have the audacity to tell Christ which sins he died for. I seriously want all of you who claim to be Christians and believe that some sin are not really sins, to stop for a second and think about how you're going to explain that concept to Christ as he sits on his judgment seat. What we are saying when we start to determine what is and is not a sin is that Christ died for nothing. That simply isn't true and is offensive to me as someone who Christ died for.

Liberals want you to believe thar sin is irrelevant and Christ died for nothing because then you are nothing. If God, who created us, does not place value in us, then who will? This concept is at the very intersection of where liberalism and Christianity collide. From the mindset of liberalism, human beings have no worth. The only value that humans have is whatever value liberals bestow upon us. It was this line of thinking that resulted in policies designed by the Democratic Party favoring abortion, eugenics and various hate crimes that we have seen perpetrated over the last 200 years. Where Christians were sending missionaries out to promote the idea that God loves the world and sent his son to die for our sins, Democrats were sending small-pox infested blankets to commit genocide against entire groups of people who they saw as undesirable.

This brings us back to the truth regarding the differences between conservative Christians and liberals. I'm not talking about the economic, political or ideological differences. I'm talking about the one overriding idea that separates conservatives from liberals and forms the basis for most of our partisan politics. Here it is: conservatives see every person as having worth and value. The root concept behind this idea is found in John 3:16. It is only logical that if God placed so much value on humanity that he sent his only begotten son to die for our sins, then we should place the same amount on value on humanity ourselves.

For the liberal, the exact opposite is true. Where conservatives Christians see individuals has having inherent value, liberals see people as nothing more than beasts of burden to be utilized by the ruling "intellectual elite" of society, which is made up of people just like them. Not only is it the liberal elite's responsibility to rule of those people, but it is their responsibility to breed those people to be the best stock available to complete the tasks the liberal elite need them to perform. This is why liberals have promoted eugenics in the past and continue to promote those same ideas though abortion today. The disregard for the value of human life is a long running core ethos of the liberal movement. This is the same belief that resulted in slavery, forced removal of Native Americans and the various purges conducted by communist and socialist regimes throughout history.

Given enough time liberals here in the U.S. will attempt those same tactics on some level. They will likely struggle to make it work, but they will try none the less. This goes to the concept I discussed in my book *Governance by Addiction* that once the liberal elite become desperate in the realization that their plan will not work, they will resort to increasingly draconian and violent actions in an attempt to force their will on the populace. The more that the liberals realize that they are losing control, the more they will rely on violence and threats in an attempt to gain and maintain control. There is no limit to the depths they will sink to in order to maintain control. Part of this is the result of sin, which helps them justify actions that anyone who was making rational decisions would know were wrong.

This difference between conservatives and liberals is important to understand because it goes to everything that the liberals are attempting to do to our society. Liberals want humanity to be stupid, poor and crippled by sin. This concept is why liberals continue to attempt to control our education system. It is why liberals continue to use public policy to keep people in debt and prevent them from moving up in society. It's also at the center of why liberals continue to attack Christians. The last thing liberals want is people who are free to make individual choices. As discussed earlier, acceptance of Jesus Christ is the first step towards individuality. If everyone was capable of making rational decisions without the interference of sin, then there would be no one for liberals to control. The more people come to know Christ, the fewer people there will be under the control of sin and as an extension, susceptible to control by liberals.

Christianity is the best tool we have when it comes to defeating the liberal ideology that envisions our enslavement and the sin nature that ultimately powers it. Let there be no doubt that sin is ultimately the genesis for all of the problems the United States is facing today. It is sin that drives the conflicts between various groups of people within our society and it is the intention of liberal elites to exploit these conflicts for their own gain. Democrats are political opportunists who will support any policy that helps them gain power and further their agenda. We see this in democratic politicians who are running for elected office and claim to hold Christian beliefs, attend church and keep the faith. However, when the votes have been tallied and they are in office they quickly revert to their old ways of supporting abortion and other ideals that have no place in the life of anyone following Christ.

Do I think that the people who go along with and vote for these elitists are evil? Not at all. I think they are people who are where any conservative would be if we did not have the benefit of enlightenment and knowledge about the truth of the sinful world around us. Most liberal voters are scared and we see that nowhere more clearly than in the phenomena colloquially referred to as "Trump Derangement Syndrome". This is no different than a person is suffering from a delusion and is confronted with the truth. The truth is scary when all that you have known is a lie. In that situation people will naturally begin to question what is true and what is false, and ultimately, they will come to a point where they will either accept the truth or decide to continue believing the lie, even if it means they have to create further lies to rationalize their belief. This is a condition known as a fix or permanent delusion and is virtually impossible to overcome. They are simply the product of the political system that essentially programed them. They aren't thinking for themselves, but engaged in the most extreme form of group think that can occur.

Liberalism is all about group think and the far-left will use any means necessary to ensure that people are not allowed to think for themselves. The most obvious case for this is the liberal control of the media. For the far-left, the media is not only a means of providing information to their followers, but a means of controlling what information is available. This is exactly the same way that sin twists our perspective of the truth. In this regard the far-left is the physical embodiment of sin. For liberals, the idea of lying about the reality of a situation is justified because it will advance their goals. We see this often during elections and other high-profile political issues. For liberals the end always justifies the means, as long as they can spin the media story to make them look good.

By no means is this new to our uniquely American form of politics. Since the dawning of our nation we have seen this type of propaganda in play. Following the Boston Massacre, we saw patriots and loyalists offering up vastly different opinions of what happened from two very different viewpoints. The difference there was that both side were able to have their voices heard. The incident was highly contentious, but there was still a free exchange of ideas regarding the events, even if the British hated the idea of the colonists having their own newspapers. Today, that doesn't exist as the majority of news media is controlled by the far-left and is used to promote their opinion at the detriment of any criticism of liberal policy objectives. We routinely have events transpire in our nation that go underreported, if not unreported altogether to help preserve the liberal narrative.

To compound this issue, people are so busy in our society that they don't have time to process the things they read or hear. In our instant everything society, people are left to process information at such a quick pace that much of the detail that is critical to understanding the world around us is lost, which provides an avenue for the influence of sin. The liberals have become experts at exploiting sound bites on the nightly news and in this confusing sin loves to continue to twist facts. One of the places we see this most prevalently is when dealing with gun control. I've lost count of how many times I've seen a liberal politician get in front of a camera at a news conference and pronounce the horrors of gun violence and the need to ban firearms. They inevitably talk about how easy it is for someone to acquire a military grade firearm and commit a mass shooting. Unfortunately, that is the message that leads off the nightly news, even if it is 100% inaccurate.

The ultimate example of bogus claims in recent years has to be the continuing liberal obsession with the Trump-Russia collusion scandal. I have yet to see a single piece of evidence that President Trump in any way colluded with the Russian government to rig the 2016 election. I have looked through all of the publicly available evidence presented to Congress and there is nothing in there to prove their case. This resulted in Congress wasting taxpayer's money attempting to impeach President Trump for a telephone call. There was no evidence ever presented in the House of Representatives that even came close to raising to the level of a "high crime or misdemeanor" as required by the Constitution. To make matters worse, the impeachment charges, Abuse of

Power and Obstructing Congress, are not even criminal acts. Nothing from this liberal insanity does more to exemplify the sinful level liberals will go to in order to lie to the U.S. citizens than Rep. Adam Schiff's completely bogus "reading" of the transcript of the phone call between President Trump and Ukrainian President Zelensky.

I can think of nothing that has occurred in the history of our nation that does more to illustrate how much sin has broken our nation than the absolute ridiculousness that was the liberals attempt to perform a coup against President Trump with a completely made up impeachment. When a sitting U.S. president can be brought to trial on charges that are not even a crime, what chance do the rest of us have when facing the wrath of the far-left? This is also where we see sin doing so much damage to our society. It is sin that tells us that convinces us to lie about someone, which promotes the ability of sin to control our lives. For our society to have any chance at a future, we must become aggressive in combatting sin when it comes to liberals and dishonesty. We must develop means of holding them accountable and making it clear that intentionally trying to deceiving the public for their own political gain will not be tolerated.

Chapter 18:
Destruction of the Collective Past

One of the interesting aspects of sin is that from the stand point of humans it is temporally fixed. By this I mean that the sin occurs at a fixed point in time, it cannot occur before or after that point. When we commit a sinful act, it does not have to carry forward with us. This is not to say that the results of the sinful act don't continue to impact our lives, but the actual action that was sinful existed at one moment in time. This is the way that God sees it, thus the reason that Christ was able to die for our sins. From the perspective of God, all the sins that you will ever commit were finite and already known at the time of Christ's death, so Christ was able to provide salvation for all people. Therefore, when we ask for forgiveness of the sin, God already knew we were going to commit the sin and the atonement has already been taken care of since God is the source of all truth. This is also why Christians don't dwell on the past sins we have committed. We ask for forgiveness, know that it has been granted and move on. The only idea I dwell on as a Christian is the people, I couldn't reach for Christ and I pray for them.

However, when a person, or group of people, refuse to acknowledge sin, they tend to carry it with them. We see this continually play out in the Democratic Party. For a party that is mired in so much hate, they continually try to either erase the hate from their history or rewrite history to make some other group responsible, generally Christians or the Republican Party. This explains why sin is the root cause of identity politics and much of the other issues that the far-left raises in society. There is no doubt that slavery was a horrible institution and that it should have ended much sooner than it did. However, the idea of reparations is equally sinful. None of the people who were responsible for slavery are still alive today. And as much as I dislike the Democratic Party and what they stand for, I'm not sure that the descendant of slaves would ever see money out of the Democratic Party. And never mind families like mine whose ancestors didn't own slaves and fought in Congress to end slavery. Why should my family be in any way responsible for reparations when our ancestors were trying to stop the Democrats from continuing slavery?

This inevitable leads to a discussion of the attempts to destroy any symbol of the Confederacy. The destruction of the symbolism

of the Confederate States is about the
Democratic Party wiping their treason
and hate from the national memory of the United
States, nothing more. This has nothing to do
with them feeling these are symbols of
oppression or hate. This is about the
Democratic Party wishing to ensure that no one
remembers the actions they undertook to
preserve the horrid institution of slavery. Just as
the far-left refuses to repent of sin, the
Democratic Party refuses to acknowledge the
horrific things they have done to this nation.

Another more sinister way that Democrats
seek to use sin to undermine our nation's history
is by attacking the foundation of our nation, the
U.S. Constitution. While I could pick any number
of examples to illustrate this point, I want to
discuss the Ninth and Tenth Amendments in
particular. Unlike the eight amendments
preceding them, the Ninth and Tenth
Amendments were not born out of the colonists'
direct interaction with the British government.
These two amendments were born out of a
conflict between Federalists and Anti-Federalists
involving the ratification of the U.S. Constitution.
At the core of the conflict was a discussion on
how well the Constitution needed to define the
limits being placed on the powers held by the
newly created federal government. The

Federalist, led by James Madison and Alexander Hamilton, argued that there was no need for the Ninth and Tenth Amendments because the limits on the powers of the federal government were already clearly defined in Article One, Section 8 of the Constitution. The Anti-Federalists, led by Patrick Henry and George Mason, argued that the large, centralized federal government created by the Constitution was potentially dangerous to the rights of both the individuals and the states, and as a result additional safeguards were needed to properly protect those rights. In the end, a compromise was reached. The U.S. Constitution was ratified with the support of many Anti-Federalists after the Federalists agreed to include the Bill of Rights which provided those additional safeguards. We need to be clear on a critical point here regarding the Anti-Federalists. The term "Anti-Federalist" was applied to the group who opposed the ratification of the U.S. Constitution in its original form, without the Bill of Rights. The "Anti-Federalists" were still federalists and both camps clearly fall under the umbrella of conservative political theory today.

The purpose of the Ninth Amendment is to simply reaffirm that the rights and powers conveyed to the federal government in the U.S. Constitution cannot be used to suppress the rights guaranteed to the citizens. For example, the Ninth Amendment makes it unconstitutional for the U.S. Congress to use the commerce clause to enact a law that would deny the Second Amendment right to keep and bear arms. Despite what the liberals believe, the Ninth Amendment does not confer any new rights that are not already enumerated in the Constitution. Unfortunately, the far-left has taken to using the Ninth Amendment as a catch all provision allowing them to create new rights out of judicial thin air.

While the Ninth Amendment doesn't get as much attention as others, it is of major important to many ongoing political battles conservatives are involved in. Beginning in the 1960s, liberal judges have adopted a twisted view of the Ninth Amendment which has resulted in a string of legal decisions displaying a level of bad jurisprudence the likes of which has not been seen in the judiciary since *Plessey v. Ferguson*. It is this twisted liberal take on the Ninth Amendment, in combination with the Fourteenth Amendment in many cases, which has served as the illegitimate legal backbone for the legalization of abortion, homosexual marriage and a number of other causes championed by the far-left.

The twisted liberal view of the Ninth Amendment has its origins in 1965 when the United States Supreme Court took up the case of *Griswold v. Connecticut*. In 1965 the court was comprised of eight progressive liberal justices appointed by President Franklin Roosevelt and one conservative justice, Associate Justice Potter Stewart, who was appointed by President Eisenhower. In *Griswold v. Connecticut* the high court used the Ninth Amendment as part of its justification to create the previously nonexistent right to access contraception and family planning services. This decision would have far reaching implications, including laying the groundwork for the 1973 *Roe v. Wade* case that legalized abortion. In his dissent, Associate Justice Stewart wrote that "…to say that the Ninth Amendment has anything to do with this case is to turn somersaults with history", and he was absolutely right.

I suspect that we will see liberals attempting to utilize their twisted view of the Ninth Amendment again in the near future in defense of the Affordable Care Act. The argument is going to be that the Ninth Amendment protects the nonexistent right to health care, when nothing could be further from the truth. Even if conservatives on the U.S. Supreme Court succeed in overturning the Affordable Care Act, and conservatives in Congress are able to create a health care reform law, the far-left is going to immediately attack the legislation utilizing their twisted view of the Ninth Amendment. As the Democratic Party moves further to the left, we will see more Socialist Democrats seeking to use this twisted view of the Ninth Amendment to pursue the right to employment, the right to financial equality and other socialist ideals. As the far-left continues their pursuit of so called "positive rights" it will be through the lens of their twisted take on the Ninth Amendment that they will seek to breathe life into these nonexistent rights.

Where the Ninth Amendment was designed to provide protections for the rights of the individual against federal over reach, the Tenth Amendment is intended to provide similar protections for the states. While I am admittedly a proponent of a literal reading of the U.S. Constitution, the Tenth Amendment is so poorly written that a literal reading is impossible. If we were to accept the Tenth Amendment as it is written, the amendment would be absolutely pointless. Clearly, the intention was to provide certain restraints on the power wielded by the federal government. As a result of this ambiguity in the Tenth Amendment, we are forced to adopt one of two possible positions. The first position would be to leave the amendment as it is and accept a virtually unlimited level of power for the federal government. For those of us with conservative political beliefs, this position is unacceptable. A government with almost absolute power leaves us in a position that is the same, if not worse, than the position we were in when the Declaration of Independence was signed in 1776. In essence leaving the Tenth Amendment to stand as is would leave us with a corrupt federal government that was constitutionally enabled to empower its own corruption. This is the sinful ideal that the far-left desires.

The second position would be to interpret the Tenth Amendment through the lens of the spirit that the Founding Fathers intended. What this means is that we recognize the need of the federal government to have some flexibility in creating policy in order for the government to function, but we also recognize that the government's power cannot be allowed to extend so far as to interfere with the rights of the states to govern effectively. I believe that the Tenth Amendment is trying to convey is a basic concept of contract law. If the Constitution does not grant a power to the federal government, then the default setting is for the power to be granted to either the states or the people, as the law allows. I believe that had our Founding Fathers known the kinds of issues we would be dealing with today involving socialism and other oppressive political beliefs attempting to take hold in our society, the Tenth Amendment would be much more reflective of this interpretation.

There have been some bright spots regarding the Tenth Amendment. The courts have for the most part been supportive of the idea that the Tenth Amendment prevents the government from forcing its will on the individual states. In recent years a federal appeals court upheld the Kansas Second Amendment Protection Act, in part on the grounds that the Tenth Amendment prevented the federal government from forcing states to execute federal laws. While the far-left hates that these kinds of laws are upheld in the courts, it makes sense that they are. Liberals always point to both the "Necessary and Proper Clause" and the "Commerce Clause" as justification for federal gun control laws. The problem is, not only does the U.S. Constitution fail to delegate the power to control firearms to the federal government, it expressly forbids the power in the Second Amendment along with an implied denial in the Ninth Amendment.

Both the "Necessary and Proper Clause" and the "Commerce Clause" cannot violate the "Supremacy Clause" found in Article Six. The "Supremacy Clause reads as follows:

> This Constitution, and the Laws of the United States which shall be made in Pursuance thereof; and all Treaties made, or which shall be made, under the Authority of the United States, shall be the supreme Law of the Land; and the Judges in every State shall be bound thereby, any Thing in the Constitution or Laws of any State to the Contrary notwithstanding.

What this means is that the U.S. Constitution, the laws passed by Congress and the treaties the United States enters into are considered the "law of the land" and all judges are required to enforce the law as such, except when doing so would be in conflict with the U.S. Constitution or an existing state law. The "Supremacy Clause" is very clear that in a conflict between a federal law and either the U.S. Constitution or an existing state law, the U.S. Constitution or the existing state law bear supremacy.

In the years to come, the Tenth Amendment will become a major battleground for conservatives. The far-left is going to make every attempt to utilize both the "Necessary and Proper Clause" and the "Commerce Clause" as weapons to force their socialist agenda upon our nation. If the laws the far-left proposes are allowed to pass they will be crippling to our nation's economy. For years we've had strong conservative attorney generals at the state level who have been quietly leading this fight. Not only do we need to join them in this fight, but we need to make sure they know that we appreciate the work they have done so far.

I have no doubt that if Madison and Hamilton were alive today, they would look at the state of our government and readily admit that the Anti-Federalists were justified in their concerns. To be completely honest, the thought of liberals governing our nation under a U.S. Constitution devoid of the Bill of Rights sends chills down my spine. Madison and Hamilton would look at our government today and recognize the legitimate need for the Bill of Rights. However, I believe they would also look at what liberals have done with the Ninth and Tenth Amendments, and see their fears about the Bill of Rights had come true. The Federalists opposed the Bill of Rights because they feared that enumerating specific rights might create a condition where the powers conveyed to the government could be expanded far beyond what the framers intended. There can be no doubt that the far-left has used the Ninth and Tenth Amendments to make that fear a reality and will continue to do so if left unchecked. This is what happens when sin is allowed to control someone's thought process.

Conclusion

In the course of this book I have discussed a lot of ways that sin impacts our lives and why the sinful nature of humans will prevent us from ever creating a government that can meet our needs as a society. However, in the introduction I promised to provide you with the answer to finding a safe space in all of this sin and chaos. The good news is this: sin has already lost. Despite all of the sinful nonsense liberals attempt to force on us, their plans will ultimately fail.

Sometime years back, I was at a local convenience store getting something to drink. As I walked back to my vehicle, I noticed a car sitting in the parking lot with a stick on its back window with the phrase "We won't let hate win" and symbols associated with the LGBTQ movement. As I sat in my vehicle preparing to leave, I took a moment to ponder the incredibly arrogant and naïve message on the sticker. In my pondering I discovered two important realizations. First, the only hate being put forth in this matter is from those who claim to be the victims of hate. God does not hate anyone. God loves the sinner and the saved alike. Rather, it is the person who desires to continue living in sin who hates God and refuse to accept His love for them. Secondly, is the ridicules notion that somehow there is something left to "win". Sin already lost at the Cross. The battle is over, the war has been won, and the victor, Jesus Christ, has been crowned and is seated at the right hand of the Father. All of this whining and complaining is doing nothing more than perpetuating the misery people are inflicting on themselves. It is not the government or religions job to be codependent to, or enablers of, the sinful behavior that is holding humanity back from progress.

The fact is that we live in a sinful, fallen world and as a result evil will win some battles from time to time. But as a follower of Jesus Christ I take comfort knowing that my king has already won the war. He didn't need a gun, a knife or sword. He didn't pick up a weapon of mass destruction. Instead he took up a cross and turned it into a symbol of mass salvation. We have nothing left to fear when we walk with Christ. The worst anyone can do to us is send destroy our flesh and blood bodies which would result in our transformation into what God wants us to really be.

This realization opens up a number of truths to those who by faith believe and follow Christ. First and foremost, we've learned that the only answer to the issue of sin is faith in Jesus Christ and his finished work at the cross. There is no other way for a person to be saved except by grace through faith. While I already discussed this realization in chapter 4, it bears repeating here. The only way to begin to counteract the destructive effects of sin in a person's life is to accept Jesus Christ. There is no way you will ever be able to live your life free from sin on your own. Christ made the sacrifice for you, so now is the time to accept the free gift of salvation and move on with your life.

I understand that there are people who will not see the need for Christ in their lives. I understand that there are people who think they can handle life on their own. However, the reality of life is very different than how they perceive life to be. The truth is that sin dramatically changes the way we perceive the world around us. Without the inner working of the Holy Spirit in our lives to help us make proper decisions, we are left adrift like a ship without a rudder, cast about by the storms of life until we finally run aground and break apart.

The anchor in the storm is Christ and without Christ to serve as the anchor your fate is sealed.

Secondly, we've learned that overcoming sin is a lifelong task that takes commitment. Sin is all around us and it's not going away until Christ returns. We must learn to live with the realization that we live in a sinful world and adjust our thoughts and behaviors to reflect this reality. Living in this sinful world is a complicated task that requires multiple approaches to achieve. However, as Christ himself said in Luke 14:27-33:

> And whosoever doth not bear his cross, and come after me, cannot be my disciple. For which of you, intending to build a tower, sitteth not down first, and counteth the cost, whether he have sufficient to finish it? Lest haply, after he hath laid the foundation, and is not able to finish it, all that behold it begin to mock him, Saying, This man began to build, and was not able to finish. Or what king, going to make war against another king, sitteth not down first, and consulteth whether he be able with ten thousand to meet him that cometh against him with twenty thousand? Or else, while the other is yet a great way off, he sendeth an ambassage, and desireth conditions of

peace. So likewise, whosoever he be of you that forsaketh not all that he hath, he cannot be my disciple.

On some level most of us who have come to know Christ knew that there would be struggles as a result. Some of us have been fortunate to have avoided major struggles in life that tested our faith. Some of us have seen more than our fair share of struggles and tests of faith only to come out better for it. Some of us have been through struggles that were in part of our own creation because we disobeyed the will of God. But how we reacted to those struggles is always the result of how strong our relationship with Christ is and how much we have changed as a person since accepting Christ.

Third, we must learn to not take sin personally. In Luke 9:23 Christ taught "…If any man will come after me, let him deny himself, and take up his cross daily, and follow me." When Christ speaks here of self-denial and the Cross, He is speaking of forgiveness. One of the places in our lives where sin finds the easiest foothold is in the area of anger and revenge. The sinful response to someone hurting you is to lash out at them in some way. That could be a physical attack, or using words to get revenge. However, this isn't in keeping with what Christ taught in Matthew 5:39 "That ye resist not evil:

but whosoever shall smite thee on thy right cheek, turn to him the other also." We've all heard about turning the other cheek, but Christ really meant it.

When we allow feelings of anger and revenge to take hold in us, we are allowing sin a gateway to take up residence in our souls. Remember that once we accept Christ, we are not our own. As Paul said in Galatians 2:20 "I am crucified with Christ: nevertheless I live; yet not I, but Christ liveth in me: and the life which I now live in the flesh I live by the faith of the Son of God, who loved me, and gave himself for me." We are not living our lives for ourselves any longer, but are living our lives for Christ. When we allow anger, fear and revenge to take hold of us, we stop serving Christ and begin serving sin.

Christ didn't just give this as a simple instruction, he lived it out, even on the cross. Christ suffered on the Cross for every sin that you and I and every person since the dawn of creation will ever commit, and he held no ill will towards any of us because of it. While hanging on the cross Christ didn't scream and rant and yell about all the sins he was suffering for. Christ prayed "Father, forgive them; for they know not what they do." How many times have we suffered because of the sinful actions of someone else? And what was our response? That should be a humbling concept for any believer. The people who hurt us are, believe it or not, also part of God's prefect creation. Their decision to inflict pain on you is not completely their own choice. They are doing so because they don't know any better. Their decision process is so twisted by the influence of sin in their life, that they lack the ability to see the full ramifications of what they are doing.

When someone does something wrong towards you, resist the urge to be angry at them. Rather, look at them as a child who simply doesn't know any better. Paul makes mention of this concept when he talked of believers in 1st Corinthians 3:2 as still being in need of spiritual milk as opposed to solid food. Just because Christ called us to come to his as children, does not mean that we must remain childlike in our faith. I assure you; I have been hurt by others more times than I can count, and in ways I would never wish on anyone. Yet, I don't look on those who hurt me with anger, and I don't look to take revenge on them. I look on them with pity that they don't know Christ and lack the ability to recognize bad decisions. I look on them with the same sorrow God does, knowing that they may not ever be saved. Every soul that is lost from God's heavenly kingdom is a tragedy. As Christ said in Luke 1:7 "I say unto you, that likewise joy shall be in heaven over one sinner that repenteth, more than over ninety and nine just persons, which need no repentance." I pray every day for God to reach out to those who hurt me. While I cannot force someone to accept Christ and the gift of eternal life, I can ask God to hold nothing they did towards me against them. If someone I have crossed paths with in life fails to receive eternal life it will not be because of me.

In John 15:12-13 Christ provided a terrific description of his sacrifice when he said "This is my commandment, That ye love one another, as I have loved you. Greater love hath no man than this, that a man lay down his life for his friends." For those of us who believe in Christ, we have no need to lay down our lives, as we have been granted eternal life. However, since we have that knowledge and security, we should make it a priority to ensure that no person is denied entry into heaven because of us. While I cannot ensure every person will get to heaven, I can be mindful of my actions and do my best to make sure that my word and deeds do not prevent someone from reaching heaven.

Fourth, learn to trust in God and develop a meaningful relationship with God. Yes, resisting the destructive influence of sin in life is a difficult task, but God provides us with a helper in the Holy Spirit to both assist and teach us in how to do so. God didn't just leave us without assistance after Christ gave us his final instructions. God understands that even after accepting Christ into our lives, we still have to live in a sinful world where our natural tendencies are to trust in money, power, possessions and people at the detriment of our relationship with God. When we trust in ourselves and our ability to provide what we need, then we limit God's ability to do great things for us and through us.

Years ago, I was attending a church that was looking to merge with another church in the area due to financial problems. During the meeting where this merger was first announced I overheard two older women sitting behind me begin to talk about how excited they were for the merger since it would mean more money for the church and that they could have a new sanctuary and kitchen. I couldn't help but marvel at the comments by these two church members. Did they not realize that Christ had preached sermons on the side of a mountain and feed 5,000 people from some wicker baskets? The truth was that like many churches today who face financial issues and declining attendance, the problem is not only issues of a sinful world, but issues of faith. It's sad to see believers turn to the law and to the sinful world when they should be turning to God. This is not to say that God will not use elements in our world to bestow blessings on us. But we need to make sure that what we are doing is with God's blessing.

Finally, we need to remember that God loves us. Virtually every Christian in the world knows the words to John 3:16 by heart. God's love for us is unending, no matter how badly we mess up. Furthermore, God does not want to be distanced from us. God wants a very close, personal relationship with us, but for that relationship to develop we have to put in a lot of work. God has done his part by sending his son, Jesus Christ, to die for our sins. Now it's time for us to do our part. It's time for us to have faith that all things will work out according to God's will, which is superior to our sinful will. None of what I have written in this book is new. It all could just as easily have come from Christ's "sermon on the mount". It's time for us to put our sinful desires behind us and move forward in the teachings of Christ.

9 7 9 8 6 5 3 2 5 8 8 5 5